Spotlight on Young Children

Teaching and Learning in the Primary Grades

Holly Bohart, Heather Benson Collick, and Kathy Charner, editors

National Association for the Education of Young Children
Washington, DC

National Association for the
Education of Young Children

1313 L Street NW, Suite 500
Washington, DC 20005-4101
202-232-8777 • 800-424-2460
www.naeyc.org

NAEYC Books

Senior Director, Content, Strategy, and Development
Susan Friedman

Editor-in-Chief
Kathy Charner

Senior Creative Design Manager
Audra Meckstroth

Managing Editor
Mary Jaffe

Senior Editor
Holly Bohart

Creative Design Specialist
Malini Dominey

Associate Editor
Rossella Procopio

Through its publications program, the National Association for the Education of Young Children (NAEYC) provides a forum for discussion of major issues and ideas in the early childhood field, with the hope of provoking thought and promoting professional growth. The views expressed or implied in this book are not necessarily those of the Association.

The following are selections published previously in *Young Children* and the issues in which they appeared: K.C. Kersey and M.L. Masterson, "Teachers Connecting With Families—In the Best Interest of Children," September 2009; J. Faulk and P. Evanshen, "Linking the Classroom Environment to Learning," September 2013; K.C. Gallagher, "Guiding Children's Friendship Development," November 2013; C. Amaro-Jiménez, "Lessons Learned From a Teacher Working With Culturally and Linguistically Diverse Children," March 2014; T. Spencer and L. Hertzog, "Community Explorers: Critical Thinking Strategies for Supporting Dual Language Learners," November 2014; G. Mindes, "Pushing Up the Social Studies From Early Childhood Education to the World," July 2015; B.L. Wright, S.L. Counsell, and S.L. Tate, "'We're Many Members, but One Body': Fostering a Healthy Self-Identity and Agency in African American Boys," July 2015; Y. Axelrod, A.H. Hall, and J.C. McNair, "A Is Burrito and B Is Sloppy Joe: Creating Print-Rich Environments for Children in K–3 Classrooms," September 2015; J.L. Hoffman, W.H. Teale, and J. Yokota, "The Book Matters! Choosing Complex Narrative Texts to Support Literacy Discussion," September 2015.

The following was published previously in *Voices of Practitioners: Teacher Research in Early Childhood Education*: C.-A.J. Baker, "Investigating the Role of Interactive Technology in a Connecticut First Grade Classroom," May 2014.

The following appeared in *Developmentally Appropriate Practice: Focus on Children in First, Second, and Third Grades*: C.J. Ferguson, S.K. Green, and C.A. Marchel, "Teacher-Made Assessments Show Children's Growth," 2014.

The following is excerpted from *Supporting Students, Meeting Standards: Best Practices for Engaged Learning in First, Second, and Third Grades*: G. Jacobs and K. Crowley, "Meeting the Next Generation Science Standards," 2014.

Photo Credits

Unless otherwise noted, photographs are copyright © iStock.

Library of Congress Control Number: 2016938683
ISBN: 978-1-938113-20-8
Item 2841

Contents

Introduction

Camia Hoard

As the music slowly fades, the first grade students in Ms. Jackson's classroom put their morning work in the green bin and their pencils in the table cups, and then gather on the rug for a reading mini-lesson. When all the students are settled with their eyes on the teacher, Ms. Jackson begins. "Who has traveled on an airplane?" she asks. Hands shoot into the air and students start to call out, "Me!" "Me!" Ms. Jackson makes eye contact with Sylvia, who is quietly raising her hand. "Sylvia, where did you go on an airplane?" she asks. "The beach," Sylvia replies. "Oh, the beach. I love the beach! What beach did you go to?" Sylvia shrugs her shoulders. "Was it Florida?" Ms. Jackson asks. "Yes," Sylvia responds.

Ms. Jackson proceeds to call on a few other students to share their experiences with airplane travel. Two minutes later, she asks the students to think about a travel experience they've had, then turn to a partner and talk about it. Almost half of the class shares a beach story. After Ms. Jackson regains the students' attention, she shows them a book, notes the author and illustrator, and explains that the story is about a girl who goes on a plane to a faraway country. She notices that not all the students are paying attention. "I'll wait," she says as she patiently closes the book and waits for students to stop talking, looking around, and fidgeting.

The challenges to creating meaningful discussions in the primary classroom are many. As teachers, we want to engage students in learning and limit the time spent waiting for their attention. Ms. Jackson did what many of us do in our lessons. She planned an open-ended question related to a book, included a think-pair-share experience to draw all students into the lesson, and with good intentions, believed that her first-graders would elaborate on their exciting stories of air travel. But the students did not have many travel experiences, and more important, the story she was about to share with them was not about airplanes. It was about mourning the loss of a loved one, handling change, and being brave—situations students *can* relate to, in deep and meaningful ways.

Tapping into students' experiences and emotions provides opportunities for their input, discussion, and reflections about authentic ideas. When teachers connect content to "authentic, integrated experiences," using high-quality instruction, learning and engagement increase (Copple & Bredekamp 2009, 43). The articles in this book present some of the key elements needed to take thinking, learning, and partnerships in classroom communities to the next level to create environments where students in grades one, two, and three develop ideas, learn problem-solving skills, and collaborate with others.

We must make sure that when we have students' eyes and ears, we do something meaningful with them. We ask questions to understand students' thinking, we listen well to what they are saying, we summarize what we are hearing, and we encourage students to explain and elaborate on their ideas. We ask ourselves reflection questions: Are students sharing creative ideas? Are they explaining things to each other? To create classrooms that burst with discussions and investigations that build on what students know, challenge their thinking, and solicit their ideas, we must treat our students like capable thinkers. How does the teaching and learning that happen in our classrooms demonstrate that we value what students have to say?

To communicate to students that their contributions are valuable, and to spur the kinds of meaningful discussions necessary for deep learning, teachers can create shared thinking goals, connect content to students' experiences, and design supportive routines for thinking.

Shared Thinking Goals

One way to foster meaningful discussions with students is to set shared thinking goals. A shared thinking goal is a clearly articulated essential question, concept, problem, or task that teachers and students explore together. This goal could be determined by the need to expand students' thinking on a topic and generate new ideas, or by students' ideas about how to explore or investigate topics, such as how they can help their community or what they should do for a class performance. Shared thinking encourages students to ask questions, ponder and wonder, listen to others' viewpoints, explain and clarify their thinking, and sometimes change their ideas in response to convincing evidence. It is where the higher-order thinking skills of the Revised Bloom's Taxonomy come in to play—understanding, applying, analyzing, evaluating, and creating (Anderson & Krathwohl 2000).

For Ms. Jackson and her first-graders in the opening scenario, the shared goal for the lesson was not clear. She was not really looking to find out if her students had ever been on a plane;

she wanted to address more important questions related to the text, including "Why is change often difficult?" To engage students in such a shared thinking goal, Ms. Jackson could have started by modeling: sharing a personal reflection followed by a thought or a "wonder," which would have set the tone for a powerful discussion. For example, Ms. Jackson could have shared her experience of traveling to New York City when she was a young girl to see her father for the first time. Using a chart depicting several different emotions and matching facial expressions, she might have described her feelings and highlighted vocabulary related to her experience. She might also have shown what she did with her hands and her body while she waited to meet her dad for the first time. This would have prepared the students to engage meaningfully with the characters and story in the text.

Building on Students' Knowledge and Experiences

Teachers further develop shared thinking goals by expanding on students' experiences and ideas. Drawing out the knowledge students already have and adding content to build on that knowledge can engage students more deeply in interactions and discussions. Before reading the book, for example, Ms. Jackson might have briefly introduced one of the book's themes—change—and asked students to share their feelings from a situation in which they have faced a change. Deepening our understanding of how students think and feel, what their passions and interests and strengths are, can and should occur every day, in every lesson and in every informal interaction.

Whatever the goal, we must engage students in thinking about the question or problem, why it is important, and how it is connected to what is happening in their world. Enlisting students as collaborators, teachers might brainstorm with students about how to effectively communicate their ideas, how to increase independent reading time, or how to express more clearly the ways in which a character changed in a book.

Thinking Routines

Once there is a clear goal for the discussion, and a teacher has established that the students are collaborators with her, students can engage in a thinking routine, which structures their thinking, makes it visible, and generates optimal discussion opportunities. Thinking routines are a set of questions or sequence of steps—"short, goal-oriented, easy-to-learn, and child-centered classroom strategies that extend and deepen children's thinking. They can become part of the structure of everyday classroom life" (Salmon 2010).

Ms. Jackson used a thinking routine known as think-pair-share. Other common routines include think-puzzle-explore and see-think-wonder. Thinking routines help teachers become powerful mediators of students' thinking. Using a think-puzzle-explore routine, for example, students ponder and brainstorm what they *think* they know about a topic, what questions or *puzzles* they have about it, and how they can *explore* the topic (Harvard Project Zero 2016). As they discuss their ideas, teachers notice what students wonder about and model thinking through problems and possibilities. Teachers encourage students to share their thoughts through drawing, writing, speaking, and dramatizing. Helping students visibly organize their thinking can help teachers shift from teacher-led to student-centered discussions.

When we engage students in deeper discussions with each other, students access their knowledge base and take ownership of the content. "Using the language of thinking in daily routines and conversations . . . fosters a classroom culture of thinking" (Salmon 2010).

This classroom culture reflects the belief that every teacher and every student has unique contributions to offer. The articles in this collection encourage educators to think about treating students like the capable thinkers they are.

Camia Hoard, MA, is a former master educator for District of Columbia Public Schools, where she evaluated and conferenced with more than 1,000 teachers to improve their practice. Prior to her work in DCPS, she was an elementary and early childhood teacher in Houston, Boston, and Chicago in both public and charter schools. In recognition of her dedication and success as a teacher, she was awarded the Kohl McCormick Early Childhood Teacher of the Year Award.

———————————

In "Linking the Primary Classroom Environment to Learning," Janet Faulk and Pamela Evanshen explore the significant ways the classroom environment contributes to student engagement. The authors provide four strategies that can maximize student learning.

When families are involved in school, children are more successful. In "Teachers Connecting With Families—In the Best Interest of Children," authors Katharine C. Kersey and Marie L. Masterson emphasize the value of engaging with families and offer ideas and suggestions to connect with students' first teachers.

In "A Is Burrito and B Is Sloppy Joe: Creating Print-Rich Environments for Students," Ysaaca Axelrod, Anna H. Hall, and Jonda C. McNair discuss research on the importance of print-rich environments and offer suggestions for supporting children's literacy development with functional print in classroom libraries, writing centers, and content area centers.

"The Book Matters! Choosing Complex Narrative Texts to Support Literary Discussion," by Jessica L. Hoffman, William H. Teale, and Junko Yokota, discusses choosing high-quality children's books to help children learn to process complex text during discussions. The authors emphasize that when students are engaged in interactive discussions, they interpret the texts using their varied "backgrounds, perspectives, and experiences . . . and realize that there are many possible responses to complex literature."

In "Meeting the Next Generation Science Standards: Best Practices for Engaged Learning," authors Gera Jacobs and Kathy Crowley describe how to integrate the three dimensions in the Next Generation Science Standards (NGSS Lead States 2013)—scientific and engineering practices, crosscutting concepts, and core disciplinary ideas. The authors provide guidance for helping students meet high expectations through strategies that include applying thinking skills.

Fostering students' ability to think like mathematicians is explored in Eugene Geist's "The Importance of Deep Thought in Mathematics Interactions: Why Focusing on the Answer Is Not the Answer." He discusses a shift in educators' thinking and practice that will enable students to think deeply and meaningfully about math.

Charity-Ann J. Baker's quest to understand how the students in her classroom respond to interactive technology led to her teacher research project highlighted in "Investigating the Role of Interactive Technology in a Connecticut First Grade Classroom." She discusses how interactive technology impacted teaching and learning.

Gayle Mindes reminds us of the importance of using real-world experiences to highlight the connection between social studies and social skills. In "Social Studies From Early Childhood Education to the World," Mindes explores ways teachers can prepare students to address social studies standards across grades by starting with students' interests and questions.

Children's ability to make friends affects their development in many ways. "Guiding Children's Friendship Development," by **Kathleen Cranley Gallagher**, offers ideas for designing activities that focus on children's relationships, and friendships in particular, to build a foundation of social competence and positive behavior.

"'We're Many Members, but One Body:' Fostering a Healthy Self-Identity and Agency in African American Boys" probes the "unique challenges and complex ways in which structural racism, including both implicit bias and explicit forms of racism, shapes the experiences and well-being of African American males." Authors **Brian L. Wright, Shelly L. Counsell**, and **Shelby L. Tate** challenge educators to consider the ways their beliefs and practices can promote—or inhibit—young children's self-identity, agency, and sense of community.

In "Community Explorers: Critical Thinking Strategies for Supporting Dual Language Learners," **Tamara Spencer** and **Lisa Hertzog** help clear up myths and misconceptions about children's dual language development. When teachers view students' bilingualism as a resource, they can provide opportunities for dual language learners to grapple with rich content and broaden their language capacities.

"Lessons Learned From a Teacher Working With Culturally and Linguistically Diverse Children," written by **Carla Amaro-Jiménez**, demonstrates the ways educators' "teaching practices and approach to teaching are related to the school success of students from diverse backgrounds and cultures" (Bohon, MacPherson, & Atiles 2005). Strategies for making learning and teaching more meaningful include providing think time, encouraging students to value what they know, and incorporating students' experiences into learning.

In closing, authors **Christine J. Ferguson, Susan K. Green**, and **Carol A. Marchel** look at assessments in the classroom. "Teacher-Made Assessments Show Children's Growth" provides a five-step assessment plan that gives teachers a clear picture of what students are learning and what to plan next.

Each article in this book includes information, ideas, and suggestions about teaching and learning with students. The emphasis is on *how* we use our time, opportunities, skills, and expertise to collaborate with students and how to value and celebrate their expertise.

References

Anderson, L.W., & D.R. Krathwohl, eds. 2000. *A Taxonomy for Learning, Teaching, and Assessing: A Revision of Bloom's Taxonomy of Educational Objectives.* Boston: Pearson.

Bohon, S.A., H. MacPherson, & J.H. Atiles. 2005. "Educational Barriers for New Latinos in Georgia." *Journal of Latinos and Education* 4 (1): 43–58.

Copple, C., & S. Bredekamp, eds. 2009. *Developmentally Appropriate Practices in Early Childhood Programs Serving Children From Birth Through Age 8.* 3rd ed. Washington, DC: NAEYC.

Harvard Project Zero. 2016. "Visible Thinking: Think Puzzle Explore." Accessed March 22. www.visiblethinkingpz.org/VisibleThinking_html_files/03_ThinkingRoutines/03d_UnderstandingRoutines/ThinkPuzzleExplore/ThinkPuzzleExplore_Routine.html.

NGSS Lead States. 2013. *Next Generation Science Standards: For States, By States.* Achieve, Inc. www.nextgenscience.org/next-generation-science-standards.

Salmon, A.K. 2010. "Tools to Enhance Young Children's Thinking." *Young Children* 65 (5): 26–31. www.naeyc.org/tyc/files/tyc/file/V4N5/Tools%20to%20Enhance%20Young%20CHildren's%20Thinking.pdf.

Linking the Primary Classroom Environment to Learning

Janet Faulk and Pamela Evanshen

The second-graders Ms. Barnett teaches are actively engaged in learning throughout the day. The classroom's screen door, which is designed to keep the butterflies that have just emerged from their cocoons from escaping into the hall, is the first indicator that children have opportunities to engage in active learning—in this case, the firsthand study of metamorphosis. The children sit together on the floor to excitedly share their observations.

Later, they break into small learning groups. Four children work with Ms. Barnett, a small group uses tablets to research butterflies on the Internet, and the rest of the children head to the loft and sit on cushions to read from a variety of narrative and informational texts related to butterflies. When the children hear the familiar transition music, they know it's time to put away their materials and return to the large group area for a teacher-led experience. During this direct instruction, Ms. Barnett uses the interactive whiteboard to introduce a math strategy for learning multiplication facts. The children practice this in pairs. Through partner talk and practice, they support one another until both children successfully demonstrate the strategy. Ms. Barnett concludes the lesson and sends children to work in their learning groups to apply the new strategy.

Students in the primary grades deserve quality experiences, instruction, and a physical environment that encourages children's engagement. Schlechty (2011) describes the engaged learner as one who is not only attentive but also demonstrates commitment and persistence when working on a task that has meaning and value.

High-quality instruction and authentic, integrated experiences lead children to higher levels of engagement and learning that are "more likely to stick" (Copple & Bredekamp 2009, 43). The Common Core State Standards (CCSS) for elementary grades present an interdisciplinary approach to instruction with a focus on both deep content learning and application of complex skills in math and English language arts—reading, writing, speaking, and listening (NGA & CCSSO 2010). The skills defined through the CCSS "offer opportunities for activities that lead to understanding" (Kendall 2011, 24). The physical classroom environment, when used as a tool to support teaching and learning for all children, supports teachers in fully engaging children in active learning.

Many elements of the physical environment impact the learning culture, including the shape and arrangement of the classroom, the grouping of the children in the available space, and the learning materials available for children's use (Evanshen & Faulk 2011; King-Sears 2007; Williams 2011). Teachers who use these elements strategically encourage children to participate enthusiastically in the learning process. Arranging the classroom environment to support children's focused learning—including collaboration and exploration—supports the attainment of the CCSS while maintaining the integrity of developmentally appropriate practice.

Use the Physical Environment to Support Focused Learning

An environment that reflects warmth and caring is a crucial component in supporting children's academic success (Diamond 2006). Young children come to the classroom at varying stages of readiness to learn. To demonstrate respect for all learners, effective teachers incorporate a range of meaningful experiences and lay a framework for creating trust and community. Teachers can individualize the classroom environment to provide all children—including those who are gifted, are dual language learners, and have special needs—with opportunities to learn.

Post Classroom Procedures to Support Positive Teaching and Learning

The importance of using procedures to support an environment of responsibility and respect is well documented (Boushey & Moser 2006; Wong & Wong 2009). Teachers can clearly outline two types of classroom practices with children: procedures for learning and procedures for respect and responsibility.

Procedures for learning—for example, an anchor chart created by the teacher and children that shows the steps for labeling a scientific drawing—help children complete assignments. They remind children about standards for learning and the practices associated with successfully completing a task. Procedures for respect and responsibility—such as guidelines for exploring materials and activities in learning centers—provide a framework for living and working together in the classroom. Combined, these tools lay the foundation for positive teaching and learning.

Teachers and children can create guiding principles for the classroom through whole group discussions, as represented by "Official Rules in First Grade" designed by Ms. Brickell's first grade class. Involving children in establishing guidelines allows everyone to feel included and reinforces the importance of working as a community. The teacher writes the children's suggestions and the agreed-on steps on paper or a whiteboard. Later, the teacher creates and posts anchor charts as visible reminders of the expectations that help create a sense of classroom community and ownership.

To encourage a commitment to the classroom community, teachers can include children's photos on charts. In Ms. Luppe's first grade classroom, photos of children following guidelines during gathering time remind classmates of classroom expectations. A chart listing the steps for editing a sentence might include photos of children completing each step of the process (capitalization, usage, punctuation, spelling). Connecting photo displays to learning accomplishments is especially important for dual language learners. Change the photos throughout the year, reflecting the current curriculum. Documenting children's efforts and accomplishments supports a sense of ownership in, and appreciation of, the learning.

Classroom Walls and Displays Guide Reflection and Extend Learning

Teachers and children can use the classroom walls as a teaching and learning tool (Evanshen & Faulk 2011). Displaying children's work documents, celebrates, and reinforces children's learning, and it encourages their participation in their learning community. When children's work is a meaningful representation of the content, it extends learning. Children can create vertical bar graphs to summarize data, for example, and display them in the classroom. The teacher might use these bar graphs as a foundation for showing the children alternative ways of representing the same data, such as horizontal bar graphs or line graphs. Active, collaborative learning experiences result in written, visual, audio, and three-dimensional products that provide multiple representations of content knowledge and are more useful for deepening understanding than work samples that represent one right answer. Such displays make visible children's different contributions, setting the stage for continuous learning.

Displaying photos of children engaged in learning experiences shows them they are valued members of the classroom learning community. Take photos of the children as they read, write, research, and discuss, and post them alongside writing, artwork, and other examples of their learning. Refer to the displays while engaging the children in discussions about their accomplishments and to remind them of what they did and what they learned. The displays also serve as valuable tools for sharing information with families.

Arrange the Classroom to Support Collaboration, Planning, and Exploration

Creating the most effective layout of a primary grade classroom involves more than figuring out where everything will fit. The goal of classroom design is to create and use resources to help children focus on learning. A variety of settings allows children to engage in learning. An environment that facilitates discussions in small groups, partners, and whole groups can increase communication and engagement. Arrange the environment to create clearly defined types of learning workspaces that support social learning. Tables, desks grouped in pods, or dyad seating arrangements allow children to quickly transition from passive listening to collaboration through activities such as partner talk, think-pair-share, and interactive learning.

According to Roskos and Neuman (2011), the physical environment provides insight into the cultural and academic norms of a classroom. The environment should be purposefully linked to learning. Areas with comfortable seating for partner work, for example, demonstrate that social learning experiences are valued. Centers that incorporate authentic and accessible materials invite children to interact with one another around their work. Children learn to associate different types of spaces with specific learning tasks. Classroom environments facilitate this process when they include a variety of settings for learning: strategically designed workspaces for large groups, small groups and partners, and individuals.

Large Group Spaces

The children in Mr. Alexander's third grade classroom are exploring the physical properties of the three basic types of rocks, comparing and contrasting size, shape, texture, and color. They sit in the carpeted large group area. Mr. Alexander uses the technology station next to the gathering space to access the Internet to support discussion of the essential question "How do I compare and contrast the three types of rocks?" Learning partners use the rocks displayed on the

---

Using the Environment to Support Dual Language Learners

Teachers can support dual language learners by

> Individualizing the classroom to reflect the cultures and customs of children in the class

> Posting the daily schedule with pictures or symbols

> Including photos of children on class charts

> Organizing word walls around concepts and writing the words in the languages spoken by the students

> Having designated spaces for small groups of children to encourage them to work and learn together

> Having children work in diverse groups so those who are DLLs benefit from English language role models

shelves adjacent to the gathering area to describe and categorize them based on their physical properties. The children capture their findings in their science journals and use this information to produce a brochure about the types of rocks.

Mr. Alexander consistently uses the bookcases that border the gathering area to display authentic materials associated with content area concepts. The bookcase tops are easily accessible display areas for authentic representations, visuals, and print resources related to current study topics, and a technology station next to the large group area allows Mr. Alexander and the children easy access to Internet resources. The instructional focus is clear to all children, with the tangible and visual representations of the learning supporting the dual language learners in particular. This designated gathering area lends itself to direct instruction and in-depth class discussion.

When organizing your classroom space, first consider the areas where large group instruction and class gatherings occur throughout the day. Establish these multipurpose spaces where all children can see and hear you and the other children, view the interactive whiteboard, and access other teaching tools.

In addition to supporting academic activities, the large group gathering space is a place for children to grow socially and emotionally and to celebrate learning, as illustrated in the following vignette.

> In the morning, the first-graders in Ms. Miller's classroom come together in the gathering area for a read-aloud, *Koi and the Kola Nuts: A Tale From Liberia*. In the afternoon, the book's theme of generosity and kindness to others is reinforced when the children return to the gathering area to count the money they collected during the last two months to donate to Heifer International, an organization that works with communities worldwide to end hunger and poverty.

Small Group and Partner Spaces

In developmentally appropriate classrooms, children explore, experiment, solve problems, and so on, while working with classmates. Small group and partner spaces help facilitate this participatory learning. Theorists and researchers highlight the value of social interaction during learning and identify it as one element of deep learning and engagement (Piaget [1936] 1963; Vygotsky [1930–35] 1978; Williams 2011). Teachers can arrange the classroom's physical environment to support these experiences, and can also use it to promote children's collaborative exploration of content.

Classrooms with designated spaces for small groups encourage children to work and learn together. Adding couches, benches, and small tables and chairs promotes these interactions and collaboration among small groups of children more than having children sit at individual desks.

Small group areas can also include centers, stations, and learning pads—flexible workspaces where children gather to work and learn together. Although teachers often ask children to "find a spot" to work together, using the term *learning pads* is a subtle reminder that their collaboration is about learning. Some teachers have children use carpet squares to define their learning pads, while others refer to any space occupied by two or three children engaged in a collaborative learning experience as a learning pad.

In learning centers and stations, teachers can address a variety of objectives while incorporating tasks that involve exploration and collaboration. In pairs or small groups, children might conduct observations, represent data, and create summaries of the process and findings. For example, the children in Mr. Doran's first grade class create scientific drawings of dandelions, label the parts of the plant, and write their observations in journals. This encourages cross-curricular literacy instruction with the "rich, provocative, critical reading and writing" (Calkins, Ehrenworth, & Lehman 2012, 12) called for in the CCSS.

Asking specific questions leads children to use the center materials in a way that will help them meet the goals of the activity. For example, in a learning station with math manipulatives, add learning prompts such as "How many blocks does it take to make a tower that measures four inches?" and "How many more blocks do you need to make a tower measuring six inches?" This task combines the concept of discovery with the math skills of measurement and estimation.

Additionally, centers can support integrated learning opportunities. A data collection center, for example, supports multidisciplinary studies, such as linking science with math and literacy.

Second grade teacher Mr. Lucero assigns children to heterogeneous learning teams that change regularly throughout the year. This morning, one team is working in the data collection center, which is defined by a small table and chairs, a two-tiered bookcase, and a divider created by placing large plants on the floor. The center is stocked with research materials, including measuring tools, magnifiers, a digital camera, and informational texts on the current question for study, "How much light do our bean plants need to grow?"

The team discusses its plant experiment. The children describe the plant that is growing under a paper bag, first with words ("The leaves are getting yellow") and then with data ("I measured and it grew only a half-inch this week"). One child uses the digital camera to take a photo of the plant, and another child adds a data point to the graph that charts its growth. They make predictions ("If we keep the light off our plant, it will not grow when we measure it next time and our plant leaves will be more yellow") and summarize their data ("Our plant grew two inches in the week it had light; it grew a half-inch when it was under the bag"). The responses the children record in their journals represent integrated content knowledge—in this case science, math, and literacy—and reflect their use of collaborative problem-solving skills.

Including varied, open-ended resources in learning centers and stations encourages children to develop concepts and exchange ideas. Sorting, categorizing, comparing, evaluating, analyzing, and reasoning are skills associated with the CCSS (NGA & CCSSO 2010). Children in the primary grades continue to depend on authentic materials, such as artifacts, environmental print, and concrete objects they can manipulate and explore, to develop their understanding. Learning centers are the optimum places in the classroom to display these learning materials. In addition, children need multiple representations of concepts through printed text, web-based information, informational text, photographs, and the arts in order to enrich and solidify their understanding.

Incorporating Technology Into the Classroom Environment

In small groups or as a whole class, students can

> Use tablets to research information on the Internet

> Use digital cameras for data collection and to document findings

> Create charts and graphs using software

> Use tablets and software for journal writing and logs

> Use assistive technologies as appropriate for those with special needs and/or developmental delays

Teachers can use technology to support the classroom learning environment by

> Setting up a technology station next to the whole group space to easily access the Internet to support discussion

> Using an interactive whiteboard to introduce new math strategies

> Integrating the International Society for Technology in Education (ISTE) standards into the curriculum (iste.org/standards)

> Discovering free curriculum resources (e.g., iste.org/resources/free-resources)

> Exploring a wide range of quality interactive media experiences on a variety of platforms (including literacy software, games, and technologies that go beyond drill and practice and foster children's creativity and problem solving)

> Using Web 2.0 tools for writing, collaboration, and playful experimentation

> Using interactive digital games as a way to explore math, reading, social studies, and science concepts

> Providing digital microscopes and other digital tools for investigation

> Encouraging children to become proficient in using digital tools such as cameras, scanners, recorders, and editing software

> Using technology tools such as email, blogs, or video conferencing to connect with other children in their communities or globally

> Recording children's stories about their art projects, activities, and interactions; making digital audio or video files to document their progress

> Using online resources to create class signs, schedules, and displays

Individual Spaces

Children need time by themselves to practice the skills they acquire through direct instruction and collaborative experiences. Teachers can design individual learning spaces to meet the needs, challenges, and abilities of all learners in the classroom. Students can choose from various individual learning spaces in the room according to preferences for

Reflection Questions

1. In what ways do you use the physical environment of the classroom to engage learners? What other ideas suggested in this article might you try, and how do you think students would benefit from the changes?

2. What routines might you develop with students that help develop respect and responsibility and support the teaching and learning in your classroom?

3. What types of learning workspaces can you incorporate into your classroom to support social learning? How can learning pads be used to support collaborative learning?

4. How would you design a data collection center to support learning in the classroom? What materials and technology would you include? How would you ensure the interdisciplinary benefits of this type of center?

light, sound, and space. A goal for students is to be able to choose the tools and conditions in which to practice and extend their own learning.

To meet the CCSS, all children must be proficient writers and critical thinkers who use writing to present and apply knowledge. Children can use clipboards, tablets, writing journals, reflection logs, and individual whiteboards to demonstrate understanding. Throughout the day, children use these tools in every space in the classroom, turning the whole group and small group areas into individual learning spaces.

Developmentally appropriate practice supports the concept of choice as an important component of the child-centered classroom. In addition to choice of materials, a variety of seating choices, offered where possible, interjects novelty into the physical environment and supports different learning styles. Rocking chairs, for example, allow kinesthetic learners to move. Exercise balls, pillows, stools, and beanbags let children feel comfortable and ready to learn. Offering seating choices at the computer station, for example, accommodates children who prefer to work from a softer seat, such as an exercise ball.

Conclusion

Our goal as educators is to create a culture of learning for all children. As we hold true to developmentally appropriate practice, let's elevate the level of teaching and learning to meet the high expectations associated with the Common Core State Standards. Classroom arrangement can encourage focused learning experiences for children and support collaboration and exploration. Additionally, teachers can use the physical environment as a tool to meet the learning needs of all children and create the positive social interactions that lead to high levels of engagement. When we strategically design and use the environment to reflect the principles of early childhood education, children benefit emotionally, academically, and socially.

References

Boushey, G., & J. Moser. 2006. *The Daily 5: Fostering Literacy Independence in the Elementary Grades.* Portland, ME: Stenhouse.

Calkins, L., M. Ehrenworth, & C. Lehman. 2012. *Pathways to the Common Core: Accelerating Achievement.* Portsmouth, NH: Heinemann.

Copple, C., & S. Bredekamp, eds. 2009. *Developmentally Appropriate Practice in Early Childhood Programs Serving Children From Birth Through Age 8.* 3rd ed. Washington, DC: NAEYC.

Diamond, M.C. 2006. "What Are the Determinants of Children's Academic Successes and Difficulties?" New Horizons for Learning website, Johns Hopkins University. http://education.jhu.edu/PD/newhorizons/ Neurosciences/articles/Determinants%20of%20Academic%20Success%20and%20Difficulties/index.html.

Evanshen, P., & J. Faulk. 2011. *A Room to Learn: Rethinking Classroom Environments.* Silver Spring, MD: Gryphon House.

Kendall, J. 2011. *Understanding Common Core State Standards*. Alexandria, VA: ASCD; Denver: McREL.

King-Sears, M.E. 2007. "Designing and Delivering Learning Center Instruction." *Intervention in School and Clinic* 42 (3): 137–47.

NGA (National Governors Association) Center for Best Practices & CCSSO (Council of Chief State School Officers). 2010. *The Common Core State Standards for English Language Arts and Literacy in History/ Social Studies, Science, and Technical Subjects*. Washington, DC: NGA Center for Best Practices & CCSSO. http://www.corestandards.org/wp-content/uploads/ELA_Standards1.pdf.

Piaget, J. [1936] 1963. *The Origins of Intelligence in Children*. New York: Norton.

Roskos, K., & S.B. Neuman. 2011. "The Classroom Environment: First, Last, and Always." *The Reading Teacher* 65 (2): 110–14.

Schlechty, P.C. 2011. *Engaging Students: The Next Level of Working on the Work*. San Francisco: Jossey-Bass.

Vygotsky, L.S. [1930–35] 1978. *Mind in Society: The Development of Higher Psychological Processes*. Ed. and trans. M. Cole, V. John-Steiner, S. Scribner, & E. Souberman. Cambridge, MA: Harvard University Press.

Williams, S. 2011. "Engaging and Informing Students Through Group Work." *Psychology Teaching Review* 17 (1): 24–34. www.eric.ed.gov/PDFS/EJ932186.pdf.

Wong, H.K., & R.T. Wong. 2009. *The First Days of School: How to Be an Effective Teacher*. 4th ed. Mountain View, CA: Harry K. Wong.

About the Authors

Janet Faulk, EdD, is an associate professor of education at Milligan College in Tennessee. She is an author and former elementary school principal, special education director, and elementary and preschool special education teacher. Janet's teaching and research focus is literacy and classroom environments.

Pamela Evanshen, EdD, is a professor of early childhood and chair for the Department of Teaching and Learning at East Tennessee State University, in Johnson City. She is an author and former elementary school administrator, director of NAEYC-accredited child care centers, and preschool special education teacher. Pamela's teaching and research focus is multiage education and classroom environments.

Teachers Connecting With Families—In the Best Interest of Children

Katharine C. Kersey and Marie L. Masterson

When families are involved in school, children's achievement improves, they have better social skills, and they are more successful learners (Caspe et al. 2011). But the greatest benefit of successful home–school partnerships is that children are more motivated to succeed. When families connect with their children's school, children develop positive beliefs about learning as well as a can-do spirit (Mapp & Kuttner 2013).

To connect families with school, teachers need to know the best ways to share information so they can build bridges and strong ties with families. Teachers also need to establish positive relationships to improve classroom–home communication and encourage all families to become involved.

Learning About Each Other

Parents hold widely varying views about their own involvement in school. Many are eager to collaborate with teachers and school efforts; however, some may be reluctant to connect with teachers, feel intimidated by a teacher, or be hesitant to come to a conference. One parent expressed frustration that he left a meeting at work and drove 45 minutes during the worst traffic of the day only to have just 10 or 15 minutes with his child's teacher. Other parents say that they do not feel welcome at their children's school. Some parents feel that a teacher is questioning their competence, and so when they come for a meeting they feel defensive. Parents could be anticipating bad news and may be surprised if the teacher has something nice to say.

Some families may hesitate to become involved because they feel inadequate in terms of their education, or perhaps because they are unable to read. Teachers might speak a language families don't understand or describe a child's progress in confusing educational jargon. Parents might cringe at the thought of being asked questions they're not sure how to answer. And most of all, parents don't want to feel judged for their child's problems, behaviors, or poor progress.

Teachers need to build connections with families so school encounters result in positive interactions and success for children.

The words *parents* and *families* are used interchangeably in this article to include all the people who are part of children's lives. In addition to parents, this can include grandparents, foster parents, stepparents, aunts and uncles, nannies, or anyone who is a significant part of a child's life. Each person is important to that child's success, as they support the family's values and culture.

Distrust and uncertainty work both ways. Teachers can also feel intimidated by parents. They may perceive a parent's strong personality as a demanding or accusatory attitude. Teachers may worry about being caught off guard or asked a question that is not easily handled. They could fear being judged or embarrassed. One teacher said that at the end of a parent–teacher conference, she experienced an awkward moment when she tried to shake hands with the parent, a practice she didn't know was considered disrespectful in the family's culture. She now takes the time to learn about the cultures of the children in her class. She often asks, "How can I better support your child and family?," "What values and skills would you like me to encourage and support?," and "Is there anything else you would like me or the school to do?" Setting parents at ease and helping them know that teachers want the same things they want for their children is well worth the time and energy it takes.

It is important to communicate in ways that make sense for each child's situation. Ask parents' permission to include other family members on a private class social media page, group texts, emails, and written materials. Invite all members of the child's support system to attend school and class events. Each relative and caregiver is important to children's success, as they support the children's positive development and achievement.

Connecting With Families

The positive interactions teachers use to create connections with families are in the best interest of the child and increase resilience (Cohen 2013). Effective teachers connect with families and plan ways to build strong relationships with them. For example, spending time with families at school events or being available to families and sharing information in many ways supports cooperative and productive teacher–family relationships.

The following suggestions illustrate some specific ways to build bridges and strengthen the family–teacher bond. Using strategies such as these helps families feel that they are a vital part of their children's school experience, and when challenges arise, both families and teachers can draw on the strong foundation that is already in place.

Before School Starts and at the Beginning of the Year

Send a personalized postcard to every child, welcoming him or her to the class. "See you soon at school. You'll make friends and enjoy learning!"

Call each child. Ask to talk to the child. When she gets on the phone, say, "Hello, Maria. I am your new teacher, and I look forward to seeing you at school!"

Have an open house for children and families as an orientation to school. Let the children explore the room so they will know what to expect on the first day. Talk with the children at their eye level to set them at ease. Introduce children and families who have common interests. Take a moment to thank each person for coming.

Plan a welcome meeting when the school year begins to show families that you care about their ideas and interests. Ask each family to complete a questionnaire to help you learn about each child's interests, strengths, pets, and hobbies. Ask for information about allergies and special concerns.

> **Begin the welcome meeting with a Family Introduction Circle.** "Tell us how you are related to _____ [child's name]." "Tell us something about _____ [child's name]." "What would you like to tell the group about yourself?" "Do you have something you would like to share with the children about your job, hobby, or a special interest?" Hand out copies of daily schedules, menus, and other information about the class or the school. Provide copies in the home languages of the families in the group. Plan time for families to get to know each other, and help them find ways to connect.

> **Make and share a "Me Bag" at the welcome meeting.** Bring a bag with a few personal items that are meaningful to you (a photo of your dog, a pair of ice skates, a book you are reading). Show them to families so they get to know you and the things you love. You can share the same Me Bag with the children when school begins, and ask them to bring in their Me Bags as well.

Throughout the Year

Call children at home. Leave a message during the school day. "Jamal, I am calling to say I noticed you helping Brandon on the playground today. He seemed grateful for your help." It takes 15 seconds, and Jamal may never want to erase it when he hears it. His family will appreciate it, too. Set aside a time each week to make these calls, and keep a list to make sure to include every child over the course of the school year.

Send home a "Great Moments!" certificate. Attach a digital photo to the certificate and highlight a special contribution, a kind gesture, or thoughtful words a child has used that week.

Use the phone to share news. Ask families to let you know when they are available, and then set up a schedule so they can look forward to hearing from you at a convenient time.

Be available for families to call you at a set time if they have questions or want to talk. When a child is sick, it is appropriate to call her to let her know she is missed.

Maximize technology to connect with busy families. Send positive email communications to families. "Today we painted outside. Ask Carmen to tell you what she did." Do this frequently so parents come to associate emails with memories of their children's experiences. Texting is a great option if you and the children's families are comfortable doing so. A private social media site for the class allows you to share positive experiences, videos, and photos of daily activities.

Say at least one positive thing each time you see a family member. "Danny has such a wonderful sense of humor." "Claire told me about your camping trip." "I want to tell you . . . !" Families enjoy hearing about interesting things their child has done and learned.

Using Technology to Connect With Families

> Record children's stories about their projects, activities, and interactions; make digital audio or video files to document their progress and share with families.

> Use online resources to create class newsletters, postcards, etc., to communicate with families.

> Use email and texting if families use these communication methods (attach photos when permitted and when you have time).

> Record children's activities, presentations, and special accomplishments. Attach a digital video by email or text for parents to appreciate what they see their child learning and doing. Or upload the video to the school or classroom website.

Record the positive things children do. Record them on a computer or tablet, or write them on index cards or in a notebook so you can share this information whenever you see a family member. Focus on conveying the message to families that you notice their children. Positive messages are particularly encouraging to a family whose child is struggling in school.

Encourage family volunteers. Any time you invite a family member to class, the child will feel excited and special. Encourage family members to read books to the class; talk about their culture, family traditions, or background; share some expertise, such as talking about their work as an electrician, doctor, or gardener; or tell the class about a special interest. Find creative ways for families to make meaningful contributions to the classroom that fit in their schedules (photocopying, sending in recycled materials for children to use for art, or preparing for an art, music, or dramatics activity).

Send home weekend project packs with activities for families and children to do together. One example is a blank book and a class mascot—a stuffed animal—that takes turns going home with the children. Families write in the book about what the mascot does with the family over the weekend. Children enjoy bringing home the stuffed animal and then sharing their diary entry with classmates when the mascot returns to school. This is a great way to help children with special needs, or those who are dual language learners, feel they are an important part of the class.

During Parent Conferences

Focus on a child's natural strengths. Affirm the child. Share special traits and unique capabilities you have noticed. "Luis shows compassion to his peers." "Jasmine works really hard at solving new math puzzles." A teacher can help parents see the potential in their child and encourage them to support and nurture the child's gifts at home.

Always ask family members to talk first. Say, "Tell me about your child." If the parent asks what you want to know, you can respond, "Tell me something your child did that made you smile." Such an approach lets parents take the lead and feel relaxed and open to a conversation.

Ask parents for their perspectives. Parents are experts about their child and may describe a child's strength or need. When they mention a strength, ask, "How do you support her at home?" When they tell you about a problem, ask, "How do you deal with that?"

Ask for help! If the child is experiencing difficulty at school and you think the parent needs to get involved, you might introduce your concern by saying, "There is something I'd like your help with."

Focus on one important issue. When you have concerns, choose one that you think can be helped or fixed. First identify it, and then brainstorm some solutions. Together with the family you can agree to a plan. "I will work on this at school, while you work on it at home. Let's set an appointment to get together again in two weeks." This encourages parents that working together can help their child succeed.

Present assessment results in strengths-based and nonstressful ways. Parents may not have had positive experiences in past discussions of their child's progress, and they may need reassurance about their concerns (e.g., their child's progress in reading). Describe how assessment is an important way to document, understand, and support children's progress. Explain the types of skills you observe their child developing, in language they can understand—not educational jargon. Focus on positive ways you can work together to build their child's social competence and academic strengths.

Start and end on a positive note. Begin with a constructive comment about the child, such as "Devon is now reading at the second grade level." When they hear something good first, parents are more likely to relax and know that you are on their child's side. Make sure to end with a commitment. "I appreciate and value the time that I share with your child, and I want to help him develop and learn."

Send a reminder. Call, text, or send an email the day before an appointment. "If you can't come that day, when is it convenient for you to come?"

When Parents Are Not Able to Come to School

Share successes immediately. If you have permission from parents, allow a child to call a parent during the day to tell about something great she just did. You can call also: "I want you to know that Dakota counted to six in Spanish today!"

Record children's activities, presentations, and special accomplishments. Send families a digital video by email or text so they can see what their child is learning and doing. Or upload the video to the school or classroom website.

Send home weekly information sheets. Use photos and descriptions to highlight what children are learning and doing.

Fill a class newsletter with highlights of class and community activities, information about the curriculum, upcoming class events, and positive guidance tips. Children can help write the news.

Establishing Positive Relationships With Families

Use every opportunity to connect positively with families: "I can't wait to see you and talk with you about all of the wonderful things your child is doing!" When a teacher adopts this attitude in her interactions with families, it is more likely that families will eagerly join in to support school and classroom activities for their child. Tell families what their children are learning at school, including the subject matter they are studying, what they are learning about themselves, and how well they are making new friends and learning about the world. Families need to hear how their children are becoming academically successful at school and, ultimately, what they are learning to navigate the world successfully. Teachers can give families hope and confidence that their children are well on their way to achieving that goal.

It is always in the best interest of children for teachers and families to have strong relationships. When teachers and families build connections and work together, children are more successful, both academically and socially. Strong home–school partnerships are particularly important for children with risk factors (Monti, Pomerantz, & Roisman 2014) and are essential for dual language learners (Tung-hsien, Wen, & Shan-mao 2015). Home–school partnerships can result in a lifetime of rich dividends for every child and help to ensure that all can achieve (Graves & Brown-Wright 2011).

Teachers can tell families, "I hear about you all the time. I heard what a great thing you all did together last night." These positive affirmations make families feel relaxed and proud. You, the teacher, are building bridges. You have a lasting impact on families when you share your values and your goals for their children. You empower families to help their child be successful socially and academically when you build positive connections to you, their child's teacher, and to school.

Connecting With Families of Dual Language Learners

> Use language-translation software to support communication.

> Avoid educational jargon when speaking with families.

> Take time to learn about the cultures and customs of the children in your class (for some people, shaking hands and looking directly in someone's eyes is considered disrespectful).

> Smile! It helps parents feel at ease no matter what language they speak.

> Invite family members to visit the class and share information about their home countries, cultures, and traditions.

> Send children home with bilingual books when appropriate and possible.

> Include books in each child's home language in the classroom library.

> Use technology tools to connect with other children globally using email, blogs, or video conferencing.

With time and patience, each step taken to build strong connections can make a positive difference. Review each strategy together with coteachers to energize mutual goals. Plan to add one new approach each week or each month, as you respond to each family's unique needs and strengths. Your effort will result in positive partnerships with families and better outcomes for children.

Helping families feel comfortable and understand how important they are to their child's success is the beginning of a partnership that strengthens as schools and teachers become sources for positive information and support. Through this approach to building connections, teachers create authentic relationships with families, and families become active participants in their children's success.

References

Caspe, M., E. Lopez, A. Chu, & H. Weiss. 2011. "Teaching the Teachers: Preparing Educators to Engage Families for Student Achievement." *Issue Brief of the National PTA and Harvard Family Research Project.* www.pta.org/files/Issue_Brief-Teacher_Prep_v2.pdf.

Cohen, J. 2013. "Creating a Positive School Climate: A Foundation for Resilience." In *Handbook of Resilience in Children,* eds. S. Goldstein & R.B. Brooks, 411–23. New York: Springer.

Graves Jr., S.L., & L. Brown-Wright. 2011. "Parent Involvement at School Entry: A National Examination of Group Differences and Achievement." *School Psychology International* 31 (1): 35–48.

Mapp, K., & P. Kuttner. 2013. "Partners in Education: A Dual Capacity-Building Framework for Family–School Partnerships. A Publication of SEDL in Collaboration With the US Department of Education." www2.ed.gov/documents/family-community/partners-education.pdf

Monti, J., E. Pomerantz, & G. Roisman. 2014. "Can Parents' Involvement in Children's Education Offset the Effects of Early Insensitivity on Academic Functioning?" *Journal of Educational Psychology* 106 (3): 859–69.

Tung-hsien, H., J.G. Wen, & C. Shan-mao. 2015. "Parental Involvement and Elementary School Students' Goals, Maladaptive Behaviors, and Achievement in Learning English as a Foreign Language." *Learning and Individual Difference* 39: 205–10.

About the Authors

Katharine C. Kersey, EdD, is a former professor of early childhood education and the director emeritus of the Child Study Center, Old Dominion University, in Norfolk, Virginia. She is the former chair of ODU's Department of Early Childhood, Speech Pathology, and Special Education and is a child behavior expert, parent educator, author, and speaker.

Marie L. Masterson, PhD, is associate professor of early childhood education at Dominican University, in River Forest, Illinois, and the former early childhood specialist for the Virginia Department of Education. She is an educational researcher, child behavior consultant, speaker, and author of multiple books related to behavior guidance, quality family childcare, and kindergarten readiness.

A Is Burrito and B Is Sloppy Joe: Creating Print-Rich Classroom Environments

Ysaaca Axelrod, Anna H. Hall, and Jonda C. McNair

When Erika arrives at school and enters her first grade classroom, she reads the morning message that her teacher, Mrs. Pruitt, has printed on the whiteboard at the front of the classroom and begins preparing for the day. After putting her coat and book bag in the cubby labeled with her name, she checks the board again to see whom Mrs. Pruitt has chosen as the author or illustrator of the week.

Erika discovers that this week she and her classmates will be learning about Nikki Grimes. She takes a moment to browse the numerous books Nikki Grimes has written, which are on display across the front of the whiteboard. Erika selects a book of poems titled *Meet Danitra Brown* from the display to read at her seat.

Lamar walks to the classroom mailboxes near the writing center and delivers two letters he wrote to his friends the night before at home. Shayi and Christian read the meal choices, also written on the board at the front of the classroom, and talk about whether they want to eat a burrito or a sloppy joe sandwich for lunch. Micah and Oliver stop by the sign-in bulletin board titled "Who's at School Today?" and move their names from "At home" to "At school" before settling in at their table.

All of these print-focused activities demonstrate a teacher's thoughtful plan to embed literacy throughout the classroom environment in meaningful and purposeful ways.

This article describes suggestions for creating print-rich environments in grades 1–3 and strategies teachers can use to engage children with this print. Included is an overview of the research supporting the importance of print-rich environments, followed by sections on functional print, classroom libraries, writing centers, and content area centers. The article ends with a discussion of the significance of this topic and implications for classroom practice.

The Importance of a Print-Rich Environment

Christie and colleagues (2014) write, "High-quality literacy programs require a literacy-rich environment with many materials to support children's learning" (13). Print-rich environments, therefore, are filled with many different kinds of print, such as books, magazines, writing materials, lists, charts, labels, signs, and writing samples from children and adults (Beeler 1993; Sailors & Hoffman 2011; Templeton & Gehsmann 2014). Such environments engage and inspire young learners while enhancing and supporting their literacy development. Templeton and Gehsmann (2014) argue that creating a print-rich environment should be a priority for teachers. This assertion is supported by Roskos and Neuman's (2011) assessment of the classroom environment, suggesting that "it is the environment that informs and documents the social interactions that will go on there, the encounters, friendships, and learning that will occur" and that "it shapes how teachers and students will feel, think, and behave. . . ." (110).

In her seminal studies of diverse early readers (children who learned to read before attending school and without any formal instruction), Durkin (1966) found that in addition to being read to regularly by parents, siblings, or caregivers, early readers tended to come from homes where abundant reading and writing materials were available and contact with paper and pencil was facilitated. Durkin, in fact, referred to the early readers as "paper and pencil kids." In other words, early readers came from homes with print-rich environments. While early readers are rare, Durkin's study offers important implications for ways early childhood classrooms can emulate the homes of early readers to support all young children's literacy development. Incorporating a wealth of functional print throughout the classroom promotes reading in the environment and is one important way to support literacy development.

Reading and Writing Support for Dual Language Learners

Support dual language learners by reflecting the diversity of the world and honoring their home languages and literacy experiences.

> Include predictable books, wordless books, children's magazines, and bilingual books in multiple languages in your classroom library.

> Provide individualized support in the writing center.

Functional Print in the Classroom

Functional print provides information about daily procedures, instructions, and routines (Beeler 1993; Christie et al. 2014). It is much more than decoration for classroom walls. Functional print helps children see that print is purposeful and can provide valuable information to help them carry out everyday activities. Functional print also serves as a management tool by providing information about classroom procedures and guidance for participating in classroom activities, offering children a certain level of independence. For example, in Mrs. Pruitt's classroom a sign is posted next to Blueberry, the class's Betta fish, reading, "Feed Blueberry 4 pellets," letting the children know how much to feed the class pet. Teachers can write directions about other tasks (e.g., how much and how often to water a plant) on sentence strips and display them around the room. Show-and-tell bulletin boards let children sign up to bring something from home and write about what they will share.

Charts created by the teacher and students (explaining concepts such as contractions, synonyms, and homophones) can be posted around the room so that children can refer to them when reading and writing. For example, when one of the authors of this article was a teacher, she wrote a morning message on the board every day to greet students as they entered the room. Although students would read the message independently upon entering the room, they also read it together as a class. This activity was used to teach important concepts such as letter–sound relationships, high-frequency words, and concepts about print like 1:1 matching, left-to-right directionality, and how to "read" punctuation marks. (For additional ways to include functional print throughout the classroom, see "Functional Print Suggestions" on this page.)

Classroom Libraries

Classroom libraries—integral components in primary classrooms—provide children with access to books and opportunities to read independently. Some experts contend that elementary classroom libraries should contain five to eight books per child (Christie et al. 2014); however, we believe having even more books is better and that a classroom library of 200 to 300 titles is ideal. The books should span multiple genres (e.g., poetry, fantasy, historical fiction, contemporary realistic fiction, and nonfiction) and different kinds of books in each genre (e.g., transitional chapter books, chapter books, alphabet books, wordless books, and predictable books) to accommodate the varied interests of children in any given classroom (Templeton & Gehsmann 2014). (See "Resources for Selecting Children's Literature" on page 29.) Due to the repetition, supportive illustrations, rhyme, and patterns in

Functional Print Suggestions

Author/Illustrator of the Week

Highlight a notable author or illustrator and introduce the children to that person's work. For the entire week, read books by that individual and create a spot on the dry-erase board or bookshelf that is labeled, for example, "Our illustrator of the week is Floyd Cooper. Here are of some of his books." Display 10 to 15 books by that person. At the end of each week move the books to the classroom library. Create an "Authors and Illustrators" bulletin board that features everyone studied over the course of the year. Some authors and illustrators appropriate for children in the primary grades are Donald Crews, Lois Ehlert, Denise Fleming, Douglas Florian, Nikki Grimes, Yumi Heo, Tana Hoban, Steve Jenkins, Barbara Lehman, J. Patrick Lewis, Yuyi Morales, Kadir Nelson, Dav Pilkey, Laura Vaccaro Seeger, David Shannon, Gary Soto, Duncan Tonatiuh, Mo Willems, and Don and Audrey Wood.

Lunch Choices/Meal

If children have choices for lunch, write the choices on the board. For example, "A is burrito and B is sloppy joe." If there are no choices, the teacher or a child can write the menu on the dry-erase board or in a designated location. ("Today we are having pizza for lunch.")

Helping Hands

Create a board that lists the jobs children are assigned each day. For example, list who will be the line leader, doorkeeper, pet caretaker.

Student of the Week

Create a bulletin board or space on a table or counter that highlights individual children. Include pictures of the child and information about his or her family, hobbies, birthday, special accomplishments, etc.

predictable books, these titles in particular can provide support for dual language learners. Magazines for children, such as *Ranger Rick*, *Big Backyard*, and *National Geographic Kids,* are also appropriate. Teachers can introduce children to many of these books and magazines during daily read-alouds and provide time for them to interact with these print materials. It is also important for children to see their teacher reading.

A fundamental belief of this article is that classroom environments should reflect the diversity of the world and honor children's home languages and literacy experiences, and that books play an important role in this effort. We believe that books should function as mirrors and windows enabling children to see images of themselves and others.

This belief is grounded by the work of R.S. Bishop (1990), who writes:

> Books are sometimes windows, offering views of worlds that may be real or imagined, familiar or strange. These windows are also sliding-glass doors, and readers have only to walk through in imagination to become part of whatever world has been created or re-created by the author. When lighting conditions are just right, however, a window can also be a mirror. Literature transforms human experience and reflects it back to us, and in that reflection we can see our own lives and experiences as part of the larger human experience. Reading, then, becomes a means of self-affirmation, and readers often seek their mirrors in books. (ix)

To support dual language learners, teachers can include bilingual books in multiple languages. Two examples are *From the Bellybutton of the Moon and Other Summer Poems/ Del ombligo de la luna y otros poemas de verano* (1998), by Francisco X. Alarcón, a collection written in English and Spanish, and *Going Home, Coming Home/Vê` Nhà, Thăm Quê Hu'o'ng* (2003), by Truong Tran, a story written in English and Vietnamese.

In addition to a diverse selection of books, it is beneficial to have a checkout system in classroom libraries so children can take books home to read with their families. In terms of bookshelves, it is valuable to vary the presentation of the books—traditional display style in which only the spines are visible and open-faced style to display the front covers. Also, books can be placed in crates or tubs based on topics (e.g., the solar system, riddles and jokes, weather, animals) or favorite authors or illustrators. A well-outfitted classroom library might also have a rug, comfortable seating such as beanbags and pillows, a lamp, stuffed animals, plants, book recordings, big books appropriate for students in grades 1-3, and posters celebrating reading.

Writing Centers

Writing centers are important classroom areas that provide opportunities for children to create their own texts and develop as writers. Children in the early grades are fully capable of expressing themselves through their current levels of emergent writing, including drawing, intentional scribbles, letter strings, invented spelling, and conventional spelling (Hansen et al. 2011). Writing serves many purposes for young children—for example, Temple, Nathan, and Temple (2013) state, "One basic function of writing is to put writers in touch with their own thoughts" (149). Writing also supports practical day-to-day routines. Children discover and develop writing skills through exposure to the functional and

meaningful uses of writing in their daily lives (Tao & Robinson 2005). As young children observe adults drawing, making lists, and using other literacy skills, they too begin to show interest in expressing their feelings through writing (Strickland et al. 2004). Well-designed writing centers include a range of materials that encourage children to voluntarily and enthusiastically engage in writing behaviors. (See "Writing Center Materials" on page 28.)

When teachers act as facilitators in the writing center and invite children to apply the skills they are learning during daily lessons, children have opportunities to explore print in meaningful and functional ways and engage in dialogue about print with their teacher and other children (Clark & Kragler 2005). Teachers scaffold children's writing through dialogue and modeling and help children become more confident in their independent writing. By taking time to listen and respond to children and provide interesting content to think and talk about, teachers can engage children in extended conversations that lead to new understandings about functional uses of writing (Strickland et al. 2004). This individualized support is beneficial in multiple ways for dual language learners, as suggested by Christie and colleagues (2014), who write, "Written as well as oral feedback affords ELLs [English language learners] specific information to improve their academic language" (342). Teachers can also help students learn to use specific writing strategies—such as forming alphabet letters, looking around the room to find an unknown word, or using invented spelling to write a word phonetically—by modeling how and when to use these strategies. Teacher modeling can be done during whole group lessons, times devoted to the teaching of writing, and one-on-one conversations in the writing center. To support

Writing Center Materials

Open-ended materials

> Blank paper books (lined and unlined)

> Paper (lined and unlined)

> Magna Doodles

> Tablets

> Chalkboards/dry-erase boards

> Writing tools (e.g., crayons, colored pencils, markers, chalk, alphabet letter stamps, ink pads)

> Alphabet cookie cutters

> Playdough

> Foam letters

> Scissors

> Staplers and tape

Prominently displayed lists

> Writing process poster describing the stages with illustrations or photos and child-friendly language

> List of interesting words compiled by the class

> Editing checklist

Mail center

> Mailboxes for each child

> Envelopes

> Letter templates

> Stickers to use as postage stamps

> Address labels

> Writing tools

Purposefully selected books

> Books used with past writing lessons

> Books by children's favorite authors and illustrators

> Nonfiction texts related to class topics

> Books about protagonists who write

Personalized resources

> Picture dictionaries

> Writing folders

> Story topic lists

> Family photographs

children as writers when they are at home, teachers can create a special writer's book bag filled with materials such as blank booklets, pencils, and markers that children take turns carrying home to use.

Content Area Centers

Literacy is all around us, and is a natural part of subject areas like science, social studies, math, and art. It is important for children to recognize that reading and writing happen while studying other disciplines; including literacy materials across content areas can help in this regard. Putting print materials and items used to create texts in centers—such as the social studies center (e.g., maps, paper, and clipboards for surveys) and the science center (e.g., informational texts, labeled rock collection)—stimulates children's conversations and learning in these areas while promoting reading and writing. By incorporating literacy materials into multiple content area centers, teachers extend children's opportunities to engage in valuable literacy play and to actively use print materials while learning about different disciplines. For instance, an art center could provide directions for creating works of art in the styles of famous artists. Directions for a Van Gogh painting might read, "Step 1. Observe Van Gogh's painting; Step 2. Paint swirls using different colors and let dry; Step 3. Add small brushstrokes over the swirls." Students can write about what inspired their artwork, and their thoughts can be added to their paintings and shared with peers. Children's books about art also make a valuable addition. A few suggestions include *Diego Rivera: His World and Ours* (2011), by Duncan Tonatiuh; *Meet Me at the Art Museum* (2012), by David Goldin; and *A Splash of Red: The Life and Art of Horace Pippin* (2013), by Jen Bryant.

Conclusion

In this article we offer examples and discuss strategies to help support literacy development through the creation of a print-rich environment, explicit modeling, and opportunities for literacy engagement. Children learn to be apprentices of written language through authentic, meaningful, and collaborative experiences (Lindfors 2008). Teachers in the examples presented were deliberate in their selection of print, choosing materials representative of the diversity of their classroom and society and meaningful to children's lives and experiences. The physical environments and teaching depicted engage and inspire young learners and describe practices that further the language and literacy development of young children.

Resources for Selecting Children's Literature

> **American Library Association Notable Books**
> Each year the American Library Association publishes a listing of notable books. "According to the Notables Criteria, 'notable' is defined as: Worthy of note or notice, important, distinguished, outstanding. As applied to children's books, notable should be thought to include books of especially commendable quality, books that exhibit venturesome creativity, and books of fiction, information, poetry, and pictures for all age levels (birth through age 14) that reflect and encourage children's interests in exemplary ways." www.ala.org/alsc/awardsgrants/notalists/ncb

> **American Indian Youth Literature Award**
> This children's book award "was created as a way to identify and honor the very best writing and illustrations by and about American Indians." The award criteria also stipulate that "books selected to receive the award will present American Indians in the fullness of their humanity in the present and past contexts." Two exemplary titles are *A Coyote Solstice Tale* (2009), by Thomas King, and *The Christmas Coat: Memories of My Sioux Childhood* (2011), by Virginia Driving Hawk Sneve. http://ailanet.org/activities/american-indian-youth-literature-award

> **Asian/Pacific American Award for Literature**
> "The goal of the Asian/Pacific American Award for Literature is to honor and recognize individual work about Asian/Pacific Americans and their heritage, based on literary and artistic merit." A sampling of titles that have won this award and would be appropriate for use in primary classrooms includes *Monsoon Afternoon* (2008), by Kashmira Sheth; *Wabi Sabi* (2008), by Mark Reibstein; and *The Shark King* (2012), by R. Kikuo Johnson. www.apalaweb.org/awards/literature-awards

> **Pura Belpré Award**
> The Pura Belpré Award, named after the first Latina librarian at the New York City Public Library, is given to outstanding K–12 titles about Latina or Latino experiences that are written or illustrated by Latinas or Latinos. A sampling of titles that are appropriate for primary classrooms include *Dear Primo: A Letter to My Cousin* (2010), by Duncan Tonatiuh; *Marisol McDonald Doesn't Match/Marisol McDonald no combina* (2013), by Monica Brown;

Just in Case: A Trickster Tale and Spanish Alphabet Book (2008), by Yuyi Morales; and *Iguanas in the Snow/Iguanas en la nieve* (2005), by Francisco X. Alarcón. www.ala.org/alsc/awardsgrants/bookmedia/belpremedal

> **Theodor Seuss Geisel Award**
> The Theodor Seuss Geisel Award, named for Dr. Seuss, is given annually by the American Library Association for exceptional books aimed at beginning readers. A few recipients of this award include *First the Egg* (2007), by Laura Vaccaro Seeger; *Ling & Ting: Not Exactly the Same!* (2010), by Grace Lin; *Little Mouse Gets Ready* (2013), by Jeff Smith; *We Are in a Book!* (2010), by Mo Willems; *Wolfsnail: A Backyard Predator* (2008), by Sarah C. Campbell; *Not a Box* (2007), by Antoinette Portis; and *Up, Tall and High!* (2012), by Ethan Long. www.ala.org/alsc/awardsgrants/bookmedia/geiselaward

> **Coretta Scott King Book Awards**
> The American Library Association annually grants the Coretta Scott King Book Award to outstanding titles about the Black experience that are written or illustrated by African Americans. A sampling of titles that are appropriate for primary classrooms include *Before John Was a Jazz Giant: A Song of John Coltrane* (2008), by Carole Boston Weatherford; *Underground: Finding the Light to Freedom* (2011), by Shane Evans; *Thunder Rose* (2007), by Jerdine Nolen; *Everett Anderson's Goodbye* (1983), by Lucille Clifton; *Uptown* (2000), by Bryan Collier; *Meet Danitra Brown* (1997), by Nikki Grimes; and *Mirandy and Brother Wind* (1997), by Patricia C. McKissack. www.ala.org/emiert/cskbookawards

> **Orbis Pictus Award**
> The National Council of Teachers of English grants the Orbis Pictus Award annually for outstanding nonfiction books. A sampling of titles that are appropriate for use in primary classrooms include *Actual Size* (2004), by Steve Jenkins; *Balloons Over Broadway: The True Story of the Puppeteer of Macy's Parade* (2011), by Melissa Sweet; and *A Splash of Red: The Life and Art of Horace Pippin* (2013), by Jen Bryant, illustrated by Melissa Sweet. www.ncte.org/awards/orbispictus

References

Beeler, T. 1993. *I Can Read! I Can Write! Creating a Print-Rich Environment*. Cypress, CA: Creative Teaching Press.

Bishop, R.S. 1990. "Mirrors, Windows, and Sliding Glass Doors." *Perspectives: Choosing and Using Books for the Classroom* 6 (3): ix–xi.

Christie, J.F., B.J. Enz, C. Vukelich, & K.A. Roskos. 2014. *Teaching Language and Literacy: Preschool Through the Elementary Grades*. 5th ed. Boston: Pearson.

Clark, P., & S. Kragler. 2005. "The Impact of Including Writing Materials in Early Childhood Classrooms on the Early Literacy Development of Children From Low-Income Families." *Early Childhood Development and Care* 175 (4): 285–301.

Durkin, D. 1966. *Children Who Read Early: Two Longitudinal Studies*. New York: Teachers College Press.

Hansen, J., R. Davis, J. Evertson, T. Freeman, D. Suskind, & H. Tower. 2011. *The PreK–2 Writing Classroom: Growing Confident Writers*. New York: Scholastic.

Lindfors, J.W. 2008. *Children's Language: Connecting Reading, Writing, and Talk*. Language and Literacy series. New York: Teachers College Press.

Roskos, K., & S.B. Neuman. 2011. "The Classroom Environment: First, Last, and Always." *The Reading Teacher* 65 (2): 110–14.

Sailors, M., & J.V. Hoffman. 2011. "Establishing a Print-Rich Classroom and School Environment." Chap. 10 in *Best Practices of Literacy Leaders: Keys to School Improvement*, eds. R.M. Bean & A.S. Dagen, 184–205. New York: Guilford.

Strickland D.S., L.M. Morrow, S.B. Neuman, K. Roskos, J.A. Schickedanz, & C. Vukelich. 2004. "The Role of Literacy in Early Childhood Education." Distinguished Educator column. *The Reading Teacher* 58 (1): 86–100.

Tao, L., & H. Robinson. 2005. "Print Rich Environments: Our Preservice Teachers' Report of What They Observed in Their Field Experiences." *Reading Horizons* 45 (4): 349–66.

Temple, C., R. Nathan, & C. Temple. 2013. *The Beginnings of Writing: A Practical Guide to Young Children's Discovery of Writing Through the Scribbling, Spelling, and Composing Stages*. 4th ed. Boston: Pearson.

Templeton, S., & K.M. Gehsmann. 2014. *Teaching Reading and Writing: The Developmental Approach—PreK to Grade 8*. Boston: Pearson.

About the Authors

Ysaaca Axelrod, EdD, is an assistant professor of children, families, and schools in the College of Education, University of Massachusetts, in Amherst. A former kindergarten teacher, Ysaaca's work focuses on language and literacy development of young emergent bilinguals.

Anna H. Hall, PhD, is an assistant professor of early childhood education at Clemson University. She is a former elementary school teacher of grades Pre-K–3, and her current research focuses on early childhood writing.

Jonda C. McNair, PhD, is a professor of literacy education at Clemson University. She is a former elementary school teacher of grades K–2.

The Book Matters! Choosing Complex Narrative Texts to Support Literary Discussion

Jessica L. Hoffman, William H. Teale, and Junko Yokota

Virtually all teachers in the early grades value reading aloud as an essential classroom literacy practice. Decades of research documents that reading aloud to first- and second-graders promotes development of early literacy skills and establishes a foundation for positive attitudes toward literacy (Trelease 2013; Van Kleeck, Stahl, & Bauer 2003).

Specifically, reading aloud to children builds oral language and vocabulary (e.g., Blewitt et al. 2009, Hargrave & Sénéchal 2000; Wasik & Bond 2001), listening comprehension—a precursor to reading comprehension (e.g., Brabham & Lynch-Brown 2002; Zucker et al. 2010)—content knowledge (Hoffman, Collins, & Schickedanz 2015; Pappas & Varelas 2004), concepts of print (Piasta et al. 2012), and alphabet knowledge and phonological awareness (Aram 2006; Brabham, Murray, & Bowden 2006). Equally important, reading aloud is one way to help young children acquire the language, values, practices, and dispositions of the literate world (Heath 1983).

Interacting With Complex Texts Through Read-Aloud Discussions

Not all read-alouds are created equal, however. Different approaches to reading aloud in primary classrooms have recently garnered increased attention in the United States because of the Common Core State Standards (CCSS). The standards call for all students to engage with complex texts that offer opportunities for higher-level thinking (for a discussion of complex text, see CCSS for English Language Arts, Appendix A [NGA & CCSSO 2010]). Because most children in first and second grades have not yet developed foundational reading skills well enough to independently read complex picture books, read-alouds offer the most robust opportunities for higher-level discussions of complex text to occur (IRA 2012) (see "Literacy Instruction With Complex Literature Aligned With Common Core State Standards" below).

Literacy Instruction With Complex Literature Aligned With Common Core State Standards

Below are two examples, using books discussed in this article, of ways teachers can incorporate strategies for choosing and sharing complex literature with young children in instruction, as specified in the K–5 College and Career Readiness Anchor Standards for Reading corresponding with CCSS (NGA & CCSSO 2010).

Reading Standard 6: Craft and Structure: Assess how point of view or purpose shapes the content and style of a text.

In Bob Graham's *April and Esme: Tooth Fairies*, the story is conveyed in ways that clearly communicate the sense of awe felt by the young tooth fairies on their first assignment without their parents, and the anxiety felt by the parents when they allow their children to go out on their own for the first time. Teachers can help students consider these differing points of view. During the first read-aloud of the book, support basic comprehension of the language, visuals, and plot. Follow up a day or two later with a second reading in which students are asked at different places in the text to consider whose point of view is represented and how it impacts the story—for instance, "How do April and Esme's parents feel about them collecting a tooth alone?" or "How do April and Esme feel about going out without their parents?" Students should also consider how the story might be different if it were told from only one point of view (the viewpoint of the girls or that of the parents). Teachers might even guide students to interactively rewrite part of the story from a single point of view to see how it differs from the original. Questions similar to these will guide students'

consideration of differences in points of view of characters. With continued experience, children will build toward interpretation of how point of view contributes to the content and style of texts.

Reading Standard 7: Integration of Knowledge and Ideas: Integrate and evaluate content presented in diverse media and formats, including visually and quantitatively, as well as in words.

Maurice Sendak's *Where the Wild Things Are* strongly demonstrates the way visuals and text work collaboratively to convey a story. To guide children's interpretations of the relationship between visuals and text, teachers can ask children to first examine the illustrations without reading the text and tell the story as they see it. Encourage them to go beyond the plot to consider mood, setting, and theme. Then, read the text to children without showing them the illustrations. Discuss what roles the text and illustrations separately have in contributing to understanding the whole story. For example, consider instances where the text and image are conflicting, such as when the image of friendly looking Wild Things is paired with the text "roared their terrible roars and gnashed their terrible teeth." Examine how the illustration becomes increasingly prominent and dominates the pages as the story develops, but then quickly diminishes after the climax, and words alone remain at the story's resolution. Discussions like these will support children's evaluation of text, a complex literacy skill.

Read-alouds that engage young children with complex texts rely on interactive discussions focused on interpretations of texts that may vary with the backgrounds, perspectives, and experiences of the children listening. In other words, discussing multiple interpretations of texts helps children realize that there are many possible responses to complex literature. Such discussions promote basic comprehension and have the potential to extend from basic comprehension to analysis of text elements, integration of ideas to make connections, and critical evaluation of the texts themselves and the ideas in them.

Read-aloud discussions that include complex processing of texts have been considered in terms of children's literary understanding (Hoffman 2011; Pantaleo 2007; Sipe 2000, 2007) and in studies of children's development of critical literacies (Vasquez 2010) and multiliteracies (Crafton, Brennan, & Silvers 2007). These studies reveal how teachers and children in first and second grades can work collaboratively to construct multilayered interpretations of texts in read-alouds (see "Why the Book Matters for Literary Discussion in the Early Grades" on page 35).

Characteristics of Literature That Support Complex Processing in Read-Aloud Discussions

Although how to read aloud is a frequent topic of studies in the literature, much less often researched is the issue of what to read—how the quality of literature impacts the quality of the read-aloud discussion (Teale, Yokota, & Martinez 2008). Essentially, some children's books provide more to think and talk about than others. To help children process complex texts in read-aloud discussions, it is important for teachers to first choose texts that can support complex interpretations. Although this article focuses on choosing high-quality narrative literature or stories, similar principles apply to selecting informational books. Appropriate narratives for young children contain accounts of connected events that typically surround a central problem and lead to a resolution.

The following sections outline characteristics of high-quality narrative children's literature to guide teachers' selections of texts. Each characteristic begins with a definition and explanation, followed by an example. The examples include all of the characteristics of quality narrative literature. In the interest of space, each book selection is used to illustrate a single characteristic. Also included are online and print resources to help teachers find and select complex children's literature (see "Resources for Locating Complex Children's Literature" on page 37).

Thematically Rich Issues

Theme is a broad, overarching idea in a text that is usually communicated implicitly through multiple features of the narrative, including plot, character, character actions, dialogue, and setting. Theme is considered a central literary element of narrative, and thus discussion of theme is important in building young readers' capacity to understand narratives as more than sequences of events. In some cases, the theme may be expressed as a moral, but many books appropriate for children in first and second grades express themes in more subtle and multifaceted ways, much like literature for older children and adults. Because theme is abstract and implicit, readers must engage deeply with a book to consider theme and will often interpret different themes within the same text.

Why the Book Matters for Literary Discussion in the Early Grades

The following is part of a read-aloud discussion about *Jamela's Dress* that was observed in Ms. Maddox's first grade classroom. It illustrates how children and teachers might interact in literary read-alouds. Anticipating that her students may not readily relate to the situations in the text, Ms. Maddox scaffolded the children's learning by linking an experience the children understand with the experience and emotions of Jamela's mother. The resulting connection to Jamela's mother was crucial to the children's ability to interpret the broader implications of Jamela's actions, and thus supported their attempts to interpret the complex meanings throughout the reading.

Ms. Maddox: The story opens with Jamela and her mother shopping for fabric. (Ms. Maddox reads.) "Mama was very pleased with the new material she'd found. She had worked hard to earn the money for it." (Ms. Maddox pauses.)

Ms. Maddox: Have any of you ever worked hard or done something around the house so you could earn something?

Hannah: I did it. I did it.

Ms. Maddox: What have you done, Hannah?

Hannah: I cleaned the refrigerator.

Ms. Maddox: So when you clean the refrigerator, do you earn something?

Hannah nods yes.

Ms. Maddox: What do you earn?

Hannah: A dollar.

Ms. Maddox: You earn a dollar. So, have you ever, when you clean the refrigerator and you earn all these dollars, do you ever go out and buy yourself anything special?

Hannah: Yes.

Ms. Maddox: What's something special that you bought before?

Hannah: Um, clothes for my toys.

Ms. Maddox: (to the whole group) Clothes for her toys, which I'm guessing is probably one of your dolls. So Hannah can relate to this. She said she worked really hard at home cleaning out the refrigerator, and she earns money for it. And when she earns money for it, she goes out and she buys herself something special, which is clothes for her dolls.

Ms. Maddox continues reading the story. She and the class discuss other characters and events. Toward the climax of the story, just as Jamela's mother is about to discover that Jamela has ruined her material, Ms. Maddox pauses again to prompt students' connections to the character of Jamela's mother.

Ms. Maddox: Hannah, let's go back to you. Do you remember how you said you worked hard cleaning out the refrigerator to get dollars, and you take those dollars and you buy clothes for your doll? How would you feel if [your sister] came in your room and took those doll clothes that you worked so hard for and destroyed them?

Hannah: I would be mad.

Ms. Maddox: You would be mad? (to the whole group) How do you think Jamela's mama's going to feel?

Children: (many talking at once) Mad, happy, mean, sad.

Ms. Maddox: Mean. Sad. Happy.

James: I think she feel like this (pretends to faint).

Dion: Yeah, he's right. I agree.

Ms. Maddox: I think she's gonna be, not mean, but probably a little bit upset.

Through the discussion in this example, the teacher's questioning developed her students' connection to a character, prompting them to relate a student's experience to the character's emotions at significant points in the text where skilled readers make such connections.

One book with rich thematic possibilities implied through character and plot is *The Empty Pot* (1990), by Demi. In this book, the aging emperor of China announces that the next emperor will be the child who grows a seed in a year's time. Children from all over China come to receive their seed from the emperor. A year later, they return with their flowering plants—all except Ping, who, despite his best efforts, has been unable to grow anything at all. It turns out the emperor had cooked all the seeds before distributing them. Ping, the only honest child to come before the emperor, is rewarded with an appointment as the next emperor.

The following are examples of themes in this story:

> **Sense of self.** Ping experiences both shame and pride when he goes before the emperor.

> **Doing one's best.** Though Ping appears to be unsuccessful at fulfilling the emperor's task, he does not give up.

> **Honesty.** Despite feeling incompetent, Ping brings his empty pot before the emperor amidst a sea of children with beautiful flowering plants.

Round Characters

High-quality narratives include round characters—characters who are dynamic, changing, and malleable. In contrast, flat (stock) characters are stable, fixed, and unresponsive to differences in particular events or characters. In other words, round characters are like real people—they act, think, and speak differently depending on the immediate context.

Kevin Henkes is a master of character development in children's books. In his book *Lilly's Purple Plastic Purse* (1996), readers are introduced to a self-absorbed girl-mouse character with a new purse. Lilly cannot wait to show the purple purse to other children at school, but when she shares it with them at an inopportune time, her teacher takes the purse away and says he will keep it until the end of the day. Lilly grows despondent at having her prized possession confiscated and then becomes increasingly enraged at being put in time-out. By the end of the day she is furious with her teacher, even drawing a picture depicting him as a monstrous figure. However, when her teacher hands her the purse as she leaves for the day, Lilly finds a note and treats from the teacher inside it and suddenly realizes how "small" she feels. Thus, Lilly is depicted as a round character who exhibits a range of emotions and also grows through her experience. As she becomes less self-centered, she learns to temper her emotions and behavior more appropriately for the social situation.

Integrating Technology Tips

As a class or in small groups, support students as they

> Research and report on different ALA (American Library Association) book awards (ala.org/alsc/awardsgrants/bookmedia)

> Read online book reviews and write their own or create one together as a class

> Read children's blogs posts about books and write their own (http://kidblog.org/home, www.bigbooklittlebook.com/about-us)

> Research and report on their favorite authors

Engaging, Complex Illustrations

Narrative picture books are a unique form of narrative literature in that they construct meaning through the interaction between text and illustrations. High-quality narrative picture books involve an artful, synergistic blending of text and illustration in which the meaning from the text and the illustrations are interconnected so that the whole is greater than the sum of its parts. This complex relationship between text and illustration is known as *transmediation*, and it demands constant construction and reconstruction of meaning from text to image and back (Sipe 1998). Research on children's use of illustrations to construct meaning in picture books during teacher read-alouds has demonstrated that even young children are quite capable of transmediating text and image, especially when supported by the teacher (Sipe 2007; Sipe & Bauer 2001).

The book *April and Esme: Tooth Fairies* (2010), by Bob Graham, is a sophisticated example of how an author artfully combines words and illustrations to create a rich, sophisticated narrative. This fantasy book depicts the first time two young tooth fairies exchange a lost tooth for a coin. Graham's story begins before the title page, as 7-year-old tooth fairy April is shown on her cell phone. The text, which provides her side of the conversation, indicates a request to pay a tooth fairy visit to the caller's grandson, Daniel. April, thrilled beyond belief to be asked, convinces her (ponytailed) father and her (tattooed) mother that she and her younger sister, Esme, are up to the task. After a number of tense moments on the mission to collect Daniel's tooth and deliver the coin, the sisters prevail and return home, traveling across a dangerous highway, to excited and proud parents.

Throughout the book Graham creates a subtle interplay between text and illustration. Good examples of this are the three double-page spreads in the book depicting the formidable highway, with its constant string of huge, fast-moving 18-wheelers, contrasted with the tiny

Resources for Locating Complex Children's Literature

Associations and Centers Book Lists

American Library Association—Recommended Reading
www.ala.org/tools/libfactsheets/alalibraryfactsheet23#children

American Library Association—Notable Books
www.ala.org/alsc/awardsgrants/notalists/ncb

International Literary Association/Children's Book Council—Children's Choices Reading List
www.literacyworldwide.org/get-resources/reading-lists/childrens-choices-reading-list

Barahona Center for the Study of Books in Spanish for Children and Adolescents
https://chicanolitbib.wordpress.com/2007/12/02/barahona-center

Children's Literature Review Journals, Best/Notable Lists, Blogs, and Reviews

HornBook
www.hbook.com/category/choosing-books/reviews

Kirkus Reviews
www.kirkusreviews.com

Booklist
www.booklistonline.com/book-reviews

Publishers Weekly (subscription required)
www.publishersweekly.com/pw/reviews

School Library Journal
www.schoollibraryjournal.com/article/CA6703692.html

Newspapers—Children's Book Reviews

New York Times
www.nytimes.com/column/childrens-books

Washington Post
www.washingtonpost.com/entertainment/books

Book Enthusiast Social Media Sites

Goodreads
www.goodreads.com

LibraryThing
www.librarything.com

School Libraries' Collection Development/Selection Tool

Titlewave: Collection Development by Follett
www.titlewave.com

Children's Literature Comprehensive Databases (see public or school libraries for access information)

Children's Literature Comprehensive Database
www.clcd.com/#/welcome

NoveList
www.ebscohost.com/novelist

tooth fairy cottage and the almost minuscule tooth fairies. In one illustration, the parents are shown in the lower left corner of the page while April and Esme hover in the upper right corner, framed by the white moon, "lift(ing) off into the night." Large trucks loom between these two images. The visual contrast effectively conveys the scale and danger of April and Esme's mission.

Rich Language

High-quality narrative literature includes rich and mature language—words and phrases that develop complex meaning and imagery for the reader. Such text introduces young readers to words that may be new or somewhat unknown as well as to familiar words used in new ways (e.g., figurative language). Rich language is not flowery or longwinded; rather, it is carefully crafted by the author, who chooses each word and structures each sentence to create an original, artistic, and tightly constructed text.

Jamela's Dress (1999), by Niki Daly, is the story of a young girl in South Africa who unintentionally destroys fabric that her mother was going to use to make a new dress when she gets wrapped up (literally) in her own desire to dress up. Daly carefully constructs his language to create imagery for the reader through word meanings and sound quality. For example, in a close reading of the sentence "Dreamily, Jamela swayed between the folds of material as they flapped and wrapped around her into a dress," readers feel the breeze blowing through the material, long and slow at first—"swayed between the folds of material"—followed by two short, quick snaps of wind that "flapped and wrapped" the material around Jamela, seemingly through no fault of her own. In other places, Daly fluidly infuses imagery through simile—"Down the road went Jamela, proud as a peacock." At other times, it is the simplicity of language that contributes to the meaning, such as the dawning dread readers experience when Jamela's mother calls to check on her but "there was no answer." Words and language are Daly's artistic tools to create rich images for his readers.

Engaging, Complex Plot

Plot is the series of events in a story and the relationships among the events, particularly how they relate to the narrative's problem and resolution. An engaging, complex plot interests readers and drives their desire to know what happens next, especially in relation to a story's resolution. Although older, more sophisticated readers can engage with problems far removed from their life experiences, younger children typically engage best with plots that relate to their more limited experiences and perspectives (Schickedanz & Collins 2012).

In Maurice Sendak's classic *Where the Wild Things Are* (1963), Max misbehaves and is sent to bed without his supper. His room transforms into a forest, and soon he sails into the land of the Wild Things, who name him King and honor him with a Wild Rumpus. But Max becomes homesick and returns to his house to find his supper waiting for him, still hot.

This plot essentially revolves around disobedience, frustration with parents, thoughts and dreams, and perhaps even real instances of running away—all issues that resonate in young children's lives. Sendak's text and illustrations work together in a seamless exploration of plot paralleled with character—Max's journey is both a dream of a physical journey (the plot) and an instance of an emotional journey (character). Sendak's plot prompts children to consider issues central to childhood.

Conclusion

In this article, we have provided examples of features of high-quality narrative literature that can support complex processing of texts in read-aloud discussions. The texts are not meant to be used as a short reading list for teachers, but rather as examples of the wide body of high-quality children's literature available. Children's literature that is carefully crafted with the characteristics described in this article can support read-aloud experiences through which teachers help children learn complex processing of texts. Frequent opportunities to collaboratively process complex texts in the early grades help children learn how to approach such texts both as emergent readers and, later, as independent ones, thus contributing to their lifelong development as skilled readers.

References

Aram, D. 2006. "Early Literacy Interventions: The Relative Roles of Storybook Reading, Alphabetic Activities, and Their Combination." *Reading and Writing: An Interdisciplinary Journal* 19 (5): 489–515.

Blewitt, P., K.M. Rump, S.E. Shealy, & S.A. Cook. 2009. "Shared Book Reading: When and How Questions Affect Young Children's Word Learning." *Journal of Educational Psychology* 101 (2): 294–304.

Brabham, E.G., & C. Lynch-Brown, C. 2002. "Effects of Teachers' Reading Aloud Styles on Vocabulary Acquisition and Comprehension of Students in the Early Elementary Grades." *Journal of Educational Psychology* 94 (3): 465–73.

Brabham, E.G., B.A. Murray, & S.H. Bowden. 2006. "Reading Alphabet Books in Kindergarten: Effects of Instructional Emphasis and Media Practice." *Journal of Research in Childhood Education* 20 (3): 219–34.

Crafton, L.K., M. Brennan, & P. Silvers. 2007. "Critical Inquiry and Multiliteracies in a First-Grade Classroom." *Language Arts* 84 (6): 510–18.

Hargrave, A.C., & M. Sénéchal. 2000. "A Book Reading Intervention With Preschool Children Who Have Limited Vocabularies: The Benefits of Regular Reading and Dialogic Reading." *Early Childhood Research Quarterly* 15 (1): 75–90.

Heath, S.B. 1983. *Ways With Words: Language, Life, and Work in Communities and Classrooms.* New York: Cambridge University Press.

Hoffman, J.L. 2011. "Co-Constructing Meaning: Interactive Literary Discussions in Kindergarten Read-Alouds." *The Reading Teacher* 65 (3): 183–94.

Hoffman, J.L., M. Collins, & J.A. Schickedanz. 2015. "Instructional Challenges in Developing Young Children's Science Concepts: Using Informational Text Read-Alouds." *The Reading Teacher* 68 (5): 363–72.

IRA (International Reading Association). 2012. *Literacy Implementation Guidance for the ELA Common Core State Standards.* Newark, DE: IRA.

NGA (National Governors Association Center for Best Practices) & CCSSO (Council of Chief State School Officers). 2010. *Common Core State Standards.* Washington, DC: NGA & CCSSO. www.corestandards.org.

Pantaleo, S. 2007. "Interthinking: Young Children Using Language to Think Collectively During Interactive Read-Alouds." *Early Childhood Education Journal,* 34 (6): 439–47.

Pappas, C.C., & M. Varelas. 2004. "Promoting Dialogic Inquiry in Information Book Read-Alouds: Young Urban Children's Ways of Making Sense in Science." In *Crossing Borders in Literacy and Science Instruction: Perspectives on Theory and Practice,* ed. E.W. Saul, 161–89. Newark, DE: IRA.

Piasta, S.B, L.M. Justice, A.S. McGinty, & J.N. Kaderavek. 2012. "Increasing Young Children's Contact With Print During Shared Reading: Longitudinal Effects on Literacy Achievement." *Child Development* 83 (3): 810–20.

Schickedanz, J., & M.F. Collins. 2012. *So Much More Than the ABCs: The Early Phases of Reading and Writing.* Washington, DC: NAEYC.

Sipe, L.R. 1998. "How Picture Books Work: A Semiotically Framed Theory of Text–Picture Relationships." *Children's Literature in Education* 29 (2): 97–108.

Sipe, L.R. 2000. "The Construction of Literary Understanding by First and Second Graders in Oral Response to Picture Storybook Read-Alouds." *Reading Research Quarterly* 35 (2): 252–75.

Sipe, L.R. 2007. *Storytime: Young Children's Literary Understanding in the Classroom.* Language and Literacy series. New York: Teachers College Press.

Sipe, L., & J. Bauer. 2001. "Urban Kindergartners' Literary Understanding of Picture Storybooks." *The New Advocate* 14 (4): 329–42.

Teale, W.H., J. Yokota, & M. Martinez. 2008. "The Book Matters: Evaluating and Selecting What to Read Aloud to Young Children." In *Effective Early Literacy Practice: Here's How, Here's Why*, ed. A. DeBruin-Parecki, 101–21. Baltimore: Paul H. Brookes Publishing Co.

Trelease, J. 2013. *The Read-Aloud Handbook*. New York: Penguin.

Van Kleeck, A., S. Stahl, & E.B. Bauer, eds. 2003. O*n Reading Books to Children: Parents and Teachers*. Mahwah, NJ: Erlbaum.

Vasquez, V. 2010. *Getting Beyond "I Like the Book": Creating Space for Critical Literacy in K–6 Classrooms*. 2nd ed. Kids Insight series. Newark, DE: IRA.

Wasik, B.A., & M.A. Bond. 2001. "Beyond the Pages of a Book: Interactive Book Reading and Language Development in Preschool Classrooms." *Journal of Educational Psychology* 93 (2): 243–50.

Zucker, T.A., L.M. Justice, S.B. Piasta, & J.N. Kaderavek. 2010. "Preschool Teachers' Literal and Inferential Questions and Children's Responses During Whole Class Shared Reading." *Early Childhood Research Quarterly* 25 (1): 65–83.

About the Authors

Jessica L. Hoffman, PhD, is an instructional coach for K–2 literacy in Winton Woods City School District in Cincinnati, Ohio. Jessica has worked in early childhood education as a classroom teacher, researcher, teacher educator, professional development provider, and literacy coach. Her work focuses on supporting higher-level literacies in early literacy instruction.

William H. Teale, EdD, is a professor of education, university scholar, and director of the Center for Literacy at the University of Illinois at Chicago. His work focuses on early literacy, the intersection of technology and literacy, and children's literature.

Junko Yokota, PhD, is director of the Center for Teaching Through Children's Books, and professor emerita at National Louis University. Her research focuses on multicultural literature, international literature, digital literature, and how children learn through literature.

Meeting the Next Generation Science Standards: Best Practices for Engaged Learning

Gera Jacobs and Kathy Crowley

Children are curious about the world and how things work. They love to explore and investigate, and science encourages them to do this. There is a "substantial body of research that supports the close connection between the development of concepts and skills in science and engineering and such factors as interest, engagement, motivation, persistence, and self-identity" (NGSS Lead States 2013, 6). Teachers can use students' curiosity and inquisitiveness to help them learn concepts in science and extend their enthusiasm for learning to all areas of the curriculum.

Science knowledge is critical to navigating our complex world, and it is required for students to be the innovators of the future. Therefore, a solid science education is necessary to prepare them for the future.

The Next Generation Science Standards

In 2012, the National Research Council (NRC) developed "A Framework for K–12 Science Education: Practices, Crosscutting Concepts, and Core Ideas" (NRC 2012), which outlines a broad set of expectations for students' science learning. The framework is based on current research in science and scientific learning and identifies the content and sequence of learning expected for all students in grades K–12. State-led teams, along with science educators, industry experts, and other stakeholders, used the framework to develop the Next Generation Science Standards (NGSS) (NGSS Lead States 2013).

Each standard has three dimensions, taken from the NRC framework: (1) scientific and engineering practices, (2) crosscutting concepts, and (3) core disciplinary ideas in physical sciences, life sciences, earth and space sciences, and engineering, technology, and applications of science. Whether you are using the NGSS or another set of science standards, meaningful science learning integrates all three of these dimensions (NGSS Lead States 2013).

Scientific and Engineering Practices

The NRC framework and the NGSS outline the following as scientific and engineering practices (NRC 2012, 3):

> Asking questions (for science) and defining problems (for engineering)

> Developing and using models

> Planning and carrying out investigations

> Analyzing and interpreting data

> Using mathematics and computational thinking

> Constructing explanations (for science) and designing solutions (for engineering)

> Engaging in argument from evidence

> Obtaining, evaluating, and communicating information

These practices are similar to the mathematical practices outlined in the Common Core State Standards (CCSS). As you help students gain proficiency in these practices—which involve acquiring knowledge as well as building specific skills—you also reinforce the skills students need in mathematics and other areas. For example, students develop models, make representations of what they observe, use technological tools, apply thinking skills, and ask and explore meaningful questions in math and social studies as well as in science. As students learn to ask questions; formulate possible answers or theories; collect data to investigate their theories; display their data in posters, electronic presentations, or other formats; and explain their findings to others, they follow the scientific method, which mirrors the steps involved in problem solving outlined in the box on page 43.

Children follow these steps as they explore science, solve math problems, decode words, engage in social interactions with peers, and grow in other areas of their lives. For example, third grade students could try out these steps with simple ice experiments beginning with deciding on a question they would like to investigate. One idea might be to investigate how to prevent an ice cube from melting as long as possible in the classroom or outside, or how to make it melt as quickly as possible. Once students decide what their questions are, they can formulate possible solutions to solve their problem, choose a solution to try out, and then record data—how many minutes did it take to melt in multiple trials? Students can record their data in graphs and write a short description of their findings to share with their classmates.

> First grade students who are just learning about graphs use strips of green paper to measure the growth of a narcissus stem spouting from a bulb in the classroom until it begins to flower. They take turns measuring each week, cutting the paper strip to the exact height of the stem. Each week they glue the measured strip onto a sheet of paper alongside the others to make a graph and track the plant's growth. After charting this growth for a few weeks and discussing how the graph represents the growth, students take turns measuring the plant with both the green strips and a ruler. One student charts the ruler measurements on another bar graph without the physical representation of the green paper stem. Because this graph requires more symbolic thinking (understanding the relationship between the actual ruler measurement and what is on the graph), their teacher scaffolds what the students know so they are able to create and understand more complex science and math models.

Steps in Problem Solving

1. What is the problem? (Identify the problem.)
2. What are some of the ways I can solve this? (Think about several solutions.)
3. What shall I try? (Choose a solution.)
4. Give it a try. (Experiment and test a solution.)
5. Did it work? (Decide if it solved the problem.)
6. If not, what else could I try? (Start the steps over and try another solution.)

Language and literacy skills—such as asking questions, constructing explanations, engaging in argument from evidence, and obtaining, evaluating, and communicating information—also are strengthened by engaging in scientific and engineering practices. Science offers dual language learners many opportunities to increase their language skills because discussions focus on shared experiences with hands-on materials (Michaels, Shouse, & Schweingruber 2007). Students learn new vocabulary, especially when teachers intentionally point out new words and use them multiple times in meaningful contexts. Science experiences also help students, including dual language learners, learn to identify parts of words—such as prefixes and suffixes—that provide clues to the overall meaning of a word; for example, *ovi* means "egg," *micro* means "very small," *saurus* means "lizard," and *tri* means "three."

As students engage in science experiments and investigations, recording their observations in a science notebook will improve their science and writing skills. They record the **problem** or question being explored, make **predictions** about what will happen, develop **plans** for testing their predictions, perform their experiments or investigations, analyze results of their **testing** and any data collected during the investigation, and draw **conclusions**, including what they learned and what it might mean. They can use drawings and sketches as the NGSS recommend to help describe any of these steps, adding more words as they are able.

To help students sharpen their thinking, deepen their scientific understanding, and express their thoughts, the NRC publication *Ready, Set, SCIENCE! Putting Research to Work in K–8 Science Classrooms* (Michaels, Shouse, & Schweingruber 2007) recommends that they engage in rigorous and active discussions—questioning, examining, and sharing their ideas, and sometimes changing their position based on ideas presented by others and on new evidence. Work with students to establish parameters for these discussions, such as listening carefully, expressing their ideas clearly, and respectfully questioning ideas by presenting evidence.

In *Ready, Set, SCIENCE!,* the authors suggest that when students work in groups on an investigation, each group member be assigned a role. For example, one student might lead the discussion about the groups' predictions, and others could take charge of planning, testing, or forming conclusions.

Crosscutting Concepts

The NRC framework and the NGSS describe the following crosscutting concepts (NRC 2012, 3):

> Patterns

> Cause and effect: Mechanism and explanation

> Scale, proportion, and quantity

> Systems and system models

> Energy and matter: Flows, cycles, and conservation

> Structure and function

> Stability and change

These concepts cut across all the major topic areas of the science curriculum. For example, students observe patterns in nature: baby animals and young plants look similar to their parents, but not exactly. The sun rises and sets each day, and summer follows spring. Understanding these patterns allows us to predict growth and future events. With guidance, meaningful experiences, and repetition in various contexts, students gain an increasingly deeper understanding of these concepts as they progress through the grades.

Many experiences invite students to explore these crosscutting concepts, including:

> Investigating cause and effect and energy by placing a small amount of water in a plastic film canister, adding a seltzer tablet, snapping on the lid, and observing the effect. Students can experiment with varying amounts of water and tablets.

> Exploring energy and matter by experimenting with batteries and hobby motors

> Learning about scale, proportion, and quantity by using blocks, LEGOs, or drawings to build scale models of the classroom

Disciplinary Core Ideas

Science standards are divided into core disciplines. In the NGSS, these disciplines are (1) physical sciences, (2) life sciences, (3) earth and space sciences, and (4) engineering, technology, and applications of science (see the box on page 46). The NGSS are written as *performance expectations*, describing what students should be able to do in order to demonstrate that they have met the standards. As with the Common Core State Standards for Mathematics, the NGSS focus on a few concepts, with the goal of students attaining a deeper understanding and application of these concepts. Activities to help students meet standards in each of the disciplinary core ideas begin on page 46.

Supporting Learners in Meeting Science Standards

As with other standards, the science standards outline *what* to teach, not *how* to teach. The NGSS document presents the standards in grade-level charts that include a detailed explanation of the disciplinary core ideas, the scientific and engineering practices, and the crosscutting concepts that were combined to develop each performance expectation. The three concepts are presented together to demonstrate the interconnectedness of the knowledge and practice of science. For each science standard, the chart also lists connections to specific Common Core State Standards for English Language Arts and Mathematics.

To meet the standards at an optimal level, students must actively explore practices, ideas, and concepts, not simply listen to how something is done or watch a demonstration (NGSS Lead States 2013). Offering students a number of materials that encourage hands-on investigations, such as balance scales, magnifiers, and microscopes, is therefore critical. In its position statement on the NGSS, the National Science Teachers Association (NSTA) recommends that students engage in diverse investigations that integrate the practices, core ideas, and crosscutting concepts to strengthen students' understanding of core ideas (NSTA). NSTA also suggests maintaining an atmosphere that promotes reflection, respect for logical thinking, and openness to alternate explanations that are based on research.

The table shown on page 47 provides an abbreviated version of a first grade physical sciences performance expectation from the NGSS (NGSS Lead States 2013). For students to meet this standard—"plan and conduct investigations to provide evidence that vibrating

Disciplinary Core Ideas in the Next Generation Science Standards

Physical Sciences

PS1: Matter and its interactions

PS2: Motion and stability: Forces and interactions

PS3: Energy

PS4: Waves and their applications in technologies
for information transfer

Life Sciences

LS1: From molecules to organisms: Structures and processes

LS2: Ecosystems: Interactions, energy, and dynamics

LS3: Heredity: Inheritance and variation of traits

LS4: Biological evolution: Unity and diversity

Earth and Space Sciences

ESS1: Earth's place in the universe

ESS2: Earth's systems

ESS3: Earth and human activity

Engineering, Technology, and Applications of Science

ETS1: Engineering design

ETS2: Links among engineering, technology, science, and society

From National Research Council (NRC), *A Framework for K–12 Science Education: Practices, Crosscutting Concepts, and Core Ideas* (Washington, DC: National Academies Press, 2012), 3.

materials can make sound and that sound can make materials vibrate"—they need multiple opportunities to actually plan and carry it out during experiences that scaffold their learning. Here is an example.

Students work in small groups to plan an investigation to design and make a musical instrument that vibrates and makes sounds. They consider a variety of materials, such as shoeboxes, rubber bands, water bottles, beads, and pie pans. As the groups discuss possibilities, their teacher asks clarifying questions to scaffold their understanding and promote further thought and problem solving: "What materials might vibrate the most? What could you add that would make an even louder or different sound? How could you test your ideas? What else could you try?"

The students use books and websites to research additional ideas for how they might design their instruments. The students create posters showing their designs. They revise their designs based on suggestions from others, then create their instruments. The groups demonstrate their instruments and reflect on how they were able to make the sounds. Their investigations take place over a few days, extending additional opportunities for students to further explore sound waves.

Students' designs and constructed instruments provide documentation for assessing their ability to plan and carry out investigations of vibrating materials and sounds. For further documentation and to assess their understanding, their teacher asks them to fill out a simple investigation form.

Integrated, Engaging Activities to Explore Science

To help students understand the interconnectedness of concepts, plan and implement units that address groups of science standards rather than isolated ones. Many schools find that an integrated approach and problem-based learning are effective ways to help students meet multiple science standards as well as standards in all areas of the curriculum. The NRC notes,

> Students need to work with scientific concepts presented through challenging, well-designed problems—problems that are meaningful from both a scientific standpoint and a personal standpoint. They need to be challenged to think about the natural world in new and different ways. They need guidance in adopting the practices of the scientific community, with its particular ways of seeing, building explanations, and supporting claims about knowledge. (Michaels, Shouse, & Schweingruber 2007, 149)

An integrated example: biodiversity. Look at the disciplinary core ideas as sources for meaningful questions and problems to explore. For example, a study of biodiversity, which is emphasized in both second and third grades in the NGSS, addresses a wide variety of science standards related to plants, animals, habitats, and diversity of life, as well as standards in other subject areas.

Begin a study of biodiversity by asking students to list or draw all the living things they can think of in five minutes. Record them on the whiteboard and point out the number of plants, insects, mammals, fish, and other categories they came up with. Introduce the prefix "bio" and explain that "bio" in front of a word refers to life and living things; the word *biodiversity* refers to the amazing amount of different living things on earth. Have students **make individual KWL charts** by listing what they already know (K) about the topic of biodiversity and what (W) questions they have about it. (They fill in what they learn [L] as they study the topic.) This promotes individual engagement and helps you learn each student's current level of understanding; it also builds on previous learning, helping the brain to connect and process the new information. After collecting students' individual charts, create a class KWL chart that focuses the study by exploring the questions students generated.

Go to the playground or a nearby park together and have students write down all the living things they see in the area. On another day, use Hula-Hoops or string to rope off small areas outside that pairs of students **investigate** with magnifying glasses, **recording** all the life they find, such as grasses, flowers, trees, birds, squirrels, and insects. Later, the students work to **identify** as many of these plants and animals as possible. They draw what they see, adding distinguishing characteristics, or take photos to **compare** with information in field guides or on websites such as www.bugfacts.net and www.allaboutbirds.org/guide/browse. Consider field guides that are available as books and smartphone or tablet apps, such as *The Sibley Guide to Birds*.

Sample Next Generation Science Standards, First Grade Physical Sciences

1-PS4 Waves and Their Applications in Technologies for Information Transfer
Students who demonstrate understanding can:

1-PS4-1 Plan and conduct investigations to provide evidence that vibrating materials can make sound and that sound can make materials vibrate. *(performance expectation)*

Science and Engineering Practices	Disciplinary Core Ideas (DCI)	Crosscutting Concepts
Planning and Carrying Out Investigations Constructing Explanations and Designing Solutions	**PS4.A: Wave Properties** • Sound can make matter vibrate, and vibrating matter can make sound.	**Cause and Effect** • Simple tests can be designed to gather evidence to support or refute student ideas about causes.

Connections to other DCIs in first grade: N/A

Common Core State Standards Connections:

CCSS Writing. 1.7. Participate in shared research and writing projects

CCSS Mathematical Practices 5. Use appropriate tools strategically

Source: *Next Generation Science Standards: For States, By States,* NGSS Lead States (Achieve, Inc. 2013). www.nextgenscience. org/1ps4-waves-applications-technologies-information-transfer. © 2013 Achieve, Inc.

Students gain math skills as they **gather data** on the numbers of plants and animals they see and graph their findings. Incorporate social studies and civic engagement by helping students enter their information into databases such as www.ebird.org, which maps birds worldwide in an effort to understand their habits and protect them.

Have students read about and **investigate** how changes in an environment, such as temperature extremes and excess or lack of water, can affect plants and animals. Such studies help students realize that nature is interconnected and that what happens to one species can affect others, including people. It also increases their appreciation for the amazing diversity of living things around them and ways they can help protect them.

As a culminating project, **create a class field guide** to the area, using students' drawings and/or photographs of plants and animals along with written descriptions of their distinguishing characteristics, habitats, and other information. Post the field guide on your class website so families and other classes can use it to identify local species.

The field guide can serve as an informal performance assessment. Reeves (2002) contends that performance-based assessment that takes place as students are involved in meaningful activities is more rigorous in many ways than the high-stakes paper-and-pencil tests in which students can simply guess at the correct answer. At the end of the project, have students fill in the last section of their individual and class KWL charts, which will provide another informal assessment of their learning. Reflect on the concepts students have learned and applied throughout the study.

Books about science. Providing science-related books in the classroom library and using them in the literacy curriculum is another way to integrate science into the day. Review the science standards to help you choose books. Include biographies of scientists, astronauts, and inventors, such as Jane Goodall, Sally Ride, Neil Armstrong, George Washington Carver, the Wright brothers, Louis Pasteur, Thomas Edison, Neil deGrasse Tyson, and Mario Molina, who won the Nobel Prize for his work studying the ozone layer. For times when students read on their own, promote comprehension by including a card in the book with a few questions for them to think about as they read. Encourage the development of writing skills by having students write about science-related topics, using their science notebooks to record observations or creating posters and electronic presentations on science experiments.

Science/discovery area. Another way to integrate the curriculum is to set up a science/discovery area that you change for different units of study. This area might contain magnifying glasses, binoculars, and a student microscope for close observations; a balance scale for comparing balanced and unbalanced forces; a variety of plants, seeds, tadpoles, and fish for learning about living things; and a variety of other materials to explore science concepts outlined in the standards, such as tuning forks, flashlights, mirrors, and magnets. It can also be the place to store other science equipment. A science/discovery area should offer opportunities to learn through multiple senses to promote more in-depth understanding. Adding books related to the topics makes this area another place for students to do research as part of integrated units of study, supporting their reading and writing skills as well.

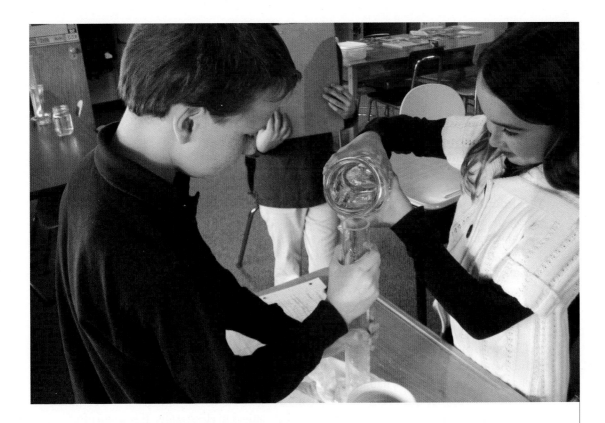

Investigations in Physical Sciences

Many primary students are intrigued by the physical sciences—topics such as sound, light, magnetism, matter, energy, force, and motion. Help students explore the disciplinary core ideas in physical science with the following ideas:

> **Compare mixtures.** Search the Internet to find a variety of mixtures for students to create and explore. Look for some recipes that require heating and others that require cooling. Here are a few ideas to try.

- Playdough recipes: Try mixing one part hair conditioner and two parts cornstarch, or two parts shaving cream and one part cornstarch. Encourage students to experiment with different amounts of the ingredients to alter the consistency of the mixture. Add washable liquid watercolors for color if desired.

- Glue: Have students design and carry out experiments to test substances that can be mixed with glue—such as liquid starch, cornstarch, and flour—to find out which glue mixtures can stretch the farthest, mold into a shape, or show other characteristics students would like to examine. This supports them as they meet standards such as the NGSS second grade standard of analyzing data from testing to determine which materials have properties best suited for a certain purpose.

> **Play thinking games.** A weekly game of 20 Questions can help students expand their thinking and questioning skills as well as deepen their understanding of matter. Place an object (or the name of an object written on a piece of paper) in a bag and ask students to guess what it is by asking yes-or-no questions about its properties—the types of material it is made of, whether it is solid or liquid, and so on. After you have modeled this several times, students can take turns bringing or choosing an object for their peers to guess.

> **Explore light.** Enlist students' ideas about how to build a light table or light box for the classroom. There are a number of suggestions on the Internet (see, for example, www. pinterest.com) that include making a basic wooden frame or using a plastic tote box, topped by translucent Plexiglas, with a light source underneath. Children can experiment with placing different materials on the Plexiglas. They can also explore shadows and flashlights. Working with these materials prepares students to meet a variety of science standards.

Investigations in Life Sciences

Use the following ideas to help students explore the disciplinary core ideas in life sciences.

> **Students' interests.** Using students' interests as a basis for learning is an effective way to help students meet standards. Subjects such as animals—of great interest to many primary students—will entice students to read informational texts and motivate them to create posters, reports, and other presentations to demonstrate what they learn. National Geographic's online magazine *Young Explorer* (http://ngexplorer.cengage.com/ ngyoungexplorer/) is equipped with an audio button that students can press to listen to a story being read. Each word is highlighted as it is read. This is especially helpful for dual language learners or students who find reading challenging.

> **Classroom pets and other animals.** Classroom pets, such as guinea pigs or fish, provide firsthand experiences for meeting many of the life sciences standards—animal adaptations, life cycles, survival needs, habitats, and similarities between parents and offspring. If a pet is allowable in your classroom, have students design a habitat for it. Discuss what animals need to thrive and what types of animals are best suited to classrooms. If you can offer students a choice of pets, ask them to research the animal they would most like to have as a class pet and write a persuasive essay about it. Have them design a presentation and give it to the class. Students can then vote on which animal they would like to have in the classroom. Discuss how students will share the responsibilities of caring for the pet. Once you have a pet, integrate its care into other learning activities, such as measuring and graphing the pet's growth over time.

> If you do not have a pet, you may be able to bring in an animal or have visits from a mobile zoo or other animal organizations, or look for websites with animal cams that students can use to see nesting birds and other animals.

> **The life cycle of plants.** Understanding the life cycle of plants, what they need to live, and adaptations that help them survive can deepen children's knowledge and appreciation of the natural world as well as help them meet science standards. Growing a variety of plants and observing them both indoors and outdoors are some of the best ways for students to learn about plants. A small space, such as a few planters on the playground, or a larger space, such as a park in easy walking distance with plants and trees, are ideal settings for learning about plants. Students can observe and record any changes they see in the trees and plants over time.

> Students might use two-liter plastic bottles or rotisserie chicken containers to make their own terrariums to learn more about plants and what they need to survive. For even more ideal conditions in which to learn and experiment, consider creating an indoor or outdoor greenhouse; search the Internet for suggestions on how to do this. There are also a number of virtual experiences that can help students learn about plants. TeacherTube and YouTube have many informative videos demonstrating the life cycle of plants. The Urban

Programs Resource Network has a number of helpful interactive videos available in both English and Spanish, such as "Dr. Arbor Talks Trees" at www.urbanext.illinois.edu/kids/.

Investigations in Earth and Space Sciences

NGSS in earth and space sciences (NGSS Lead States 2013) include the following:

> First grade: Observing and describing patterns in the sun, moon, and stars and describing the amount of daylight at different times of the year

> Second grade: Providing evidence from various sources that earth events can occur quickly (e.g., hurricanes) or slowly (e.g., erosion) and identifying where water is found on Earth

> Third grade: Making claims about solutions that reduce the impact of weather-related hazards and making tables to display typical seasonal weather conditions and climates

Use the following to help students explore the disciplinary core ideas in earth and space sciences.

> **Amount of daylight.** Students can gather data by keeping track each day of when sunrise and sunset occur and the various weather conditions. Place an indoor/outdoor thermometer where students can view it. Have them record the data on individual and class charts—on paper or in a computer file that can be projected on a whiteboard—and then graph the data each month to help them see trends.

> **Erosion.** Discuss erosion with the students and brainstorm experiments for testing the effects of erosion on soil and sand. Check websites such as www.teacher.scholastic.com/dirt/index.htm for suggestions. After students carry out several experiments, discuss ways to help prevent erosion from wind and rain. Ask students to choose two possible erosion solutions and make a poster or digital presentation showing the benefits and drawbacks of each solution; have them share their presentations with the class.

> **Earth science resources.** NASA's Space Place at www.spaceplace.nasa.gov has games, apps, facts, activities, videos, and more on a variety of topics related to earth and space science, in English and Spanish. Search the Internet for other helpful sites, such as www.kids.nationalgeographic.com/kids, www.scholastic.com/magicschoolbus/games/sciencenews/index.htm, www.weatherwizkids.com, and www.crh.noaa.gov/gid/?n=weatherforkids.

Investigations in Engineering, Technology, and Applications of Science

Science, engineering, and technology have been combined in the NGSS, enabling students to put science and math skills into practice. STEM (science, technology, engineering, and mathematics) has received a great deal of attention nationally and is seen as an important field for future jobs and opportunities. It is vital to support both girls and boys in these fields by providing hands-on activities and engaging experiences with technology that will support their interests and enhance their self-confidence.

The developers of the NGSS hope that by combining engineering design with the science standards, students will be better prepared to develop models and solutions to environmental and other challenges society faces today and in the future. The Boston Science Museum has an excellent description and graphic of the design process at www.eie.org/overview/engineering-design-process.

There are several standards in this area for primary students:

> First and second grades: Define a simple problem that can be solved with a new tool or object by asking questions, making observations, and gathering data on a situation people would like to change; develop a drawing or physical model to show how an object's shape helps it to solve a problem; compare data from tests of two objects designed to solve a problem to see how each performs

> Third grade: Define a design problem related to a need or want, including criteria for success; generate and compare possible solutions; plan and carry out tests to find aspects that can be improved in a model or prototype (NGSS Lead States 2013)

There are many ways for students to explore the disciplinary core concepts in engineering, technology, and application of science. Here are some suggestions to build their skills in defining problems and finding solutions.

> Have students work in groups to design a marble maze. The class could discuss parameters, problems they might encounter, and materials they might employ for a solution, such as LEGOs, pool noodles, cardboard tubes, or rain gutters. Students can sketch their solutions and then construct their models. Students could share their mazes, discussing benefits and problems, and then draw and construct changes to their mazes to make them more effective. This type of project is well suited to using a differentiated teaching approach, as it allows students to work at their own pace. Visit www.ciese.org/engineeringproj.html to view a variety of design problems and ideas for supporting students' efforts.

> Discuss a societal problem, such as pollution, and have students work in small groups to discuss possible solutions, such as recycling. The Internet, children's magazines, and informational text are all potential resources for their research. For example, students might explore ways to recycle paper by looking at sites such as www.pbskids.org/zoom/activities/sci/recyclingpaper.html. Small groups could discuss alternate designs for straining the water from the paper pulp, and then sketch and test out their ideas.

> Students could also work together in groups to design a solution for reducing noise pollution in their environment. After students have spent time brainstorming ideas, you might narrow their focus by suggesting they design something they might wear. Once they have a list of ideas, ask them to evaluate their designs for effectiveness, safety, and practicality.

Home–School Connections

Involve families in your science program. Provide copies of the standards you are helping the children to meet and ask family members if they have any expertise they could share. If you are able to take field trips, you could ask for suggestions of places to visit that would enhance children's science learning. Some family members may be interested in accompanying the class and leading a small group. Families are often happy to contribute materials or supplies. Some teachers make a wish list that they pass out at an open house or post on the class website. The list includes items that will be used throughout the year, such as measuring cups, batteries, cornstarch, flour, food coloring, and other ingredients for mixtures, that families might be able to donate to the class.

Send home suggestions of simple explorations families can do at home, along with a form for jotting down their process and conclusions. Knowing the students' families and their resources is essential. You might find it most beneficial to send home simple science kits that include a book and the materials needed for an activity. For example, one kit might include directions for an engineering challenge of designing and building a boat of aluminum foil that can stay afloat. Another challenge might be to add pennies to the boat and refine the design to accommodate the additional weight. Pair this activity with a few poems you provide about water from a book such as *Water Music: Poems for Children*, by Jane Yolen. This type of activity can help students learn about engineering, science, and literacy and promote family engagement. Encourage families to experience the beauty of nature together if possible and to talk about their appreciation for plants, animals, and the world around them.

Consider hosting a STEM or STEAM (science, technology, engineering, arts, and mathematics) evening and invite families to help plan this event. Set up several stations inside or outdoors that children and adults can participate in together. For example, they might build and test ramps made from PVC tubing or rain gutters and roll materials such as ping-pong balls, marbles, or miniature cars down the ramps. They could explore forces, interactions, and gravity by creating art made by filling a knee-high stocking with a cup of aquarium or pea gravel, tying it closed, dipping it in several colors of paint in a pie tin, and then dropping it on a large sheet of paper. Families could explore painting with magnets by placing a piece of paper in a shoebox, adding drops of paint, paperclips, and other metal objects on the paper, and then moving a magnet under the shoebox to create a painting. Set up a technology station with laptops and tablets that have developmentally appropriate, interactive apps and programs. At another station, students and families can sketch or create a scale model of a space station with recycled materials.

Nurturing Children's Sense of Wonder in Nature

Science isn't just about measuring and hypothesizing and problem solving. An important goal in the primary grades is to nurture children's sense of wonder and appreciation for the world. Rachel Carson (1965) expresses her wish that each child would have a "sense of wonder so indestructible that it would last throughout life" (45) and notes that "if a child is to keep alive his inborn sense of wonder . . . he needs the companionship of at least one adult who can share it, rediscovering with him the joy, excitement, and mystery of the world we live in" (55). Each teacher has the privilege of being one of the adults who can keep children's sense of wonder alive. Science can be a magnificent window into the world of wonder, and connecting students to nature is one important way to provide this. Research shows important benefits to putting children in touch with nature, including improved cognitive and observational skills and an increased sense of health and well-being (Rivkin 2014). Connecting with nature can create a buffer for stress and has even been shown to help lessen symptoms of attention deficit disorder (Children & Nature Network, n.d.).

Deepen children's appreciation for the natural world by providing opportunities to walk through a park or woods or even simply notice flowers, trees, or other living things nearby. Add a few flowerpots or a raised planter box to your school's outside area where students can plant seeds and bulbs. Add items from nature to the classroom, such as pinecones, seashells, rocks, and plants. Students' families may enjoy contributing nature items to the classrooms. Look for further resources and nature information at www.natureexplore.org.

Encourage students and families to be part of the scientific and global community that is working to improve the environment—for example, by taking part in recycling and cleanup efforts. There are also several sites where the class and the children's families can contribute data to worldwide efforts, such as the GLOBE program (www.globe.gov/documents/10157/380993/tg_intro.pdf). Here, students and families enter data such as when they see the first spring buds open in their neighborhood. Choose games and websites that promote environmental awareness and positive values, such as www.meetthegreens.org, as another way to help students make connections to the world around them.

Conclusion

Actively involving students in scientific inquiry, investigations of topics of interest and worth, and engineering design challenges can help them meet standards in all areas of the curriculum. Having a strong foundation in science will also help prepare students for future success: there is increasing demand for people who are competent in the STEM areas. The science, engineering, and technology topics you introduce may tap into students' interests, unlocking a passion for learning and a desire to learn more about an area they want to pursue. Engineering design challenges and discussions may spur an interest that could lead to students pursuing solutions to global needs, such as wind or solar power.

Through the experiences you provide, students can grow into concerned, knowledgeable citizens who want to be good stewards of their environment and preserve it for future generations. Helping students discover and explore the world beyond them aids in their social and emotional development as well, assisting them in understanding their interconnectedness with nature.

References

Carson, R. 1965. *The Sense of Wonder*. New York: Harper Row. Children & Nature Network. n.d. Website. www.childrenandnature.org/research.

Michaels, S., A.W. Shouse, & H.A. Schweingruber. 2007. *Ready, Set, Science! Putting Research to Work in K–8 Science Classrooms*. Washington, DC: The National Academies Press.

NGSS Lead States. 2013. *Next Generation Science Standards: For States, By States*. Achieve, Inc. www. nextgenscience.org/next-generation-science-standards.

NRC (National Research Council). 2012. "A Framework for K–12 Science Education: Practices, Crosscutting Concepts, and Core Ideas." Washington, DC: National Academies Press.

NSTA (National Science Teachers Association). 2013. "The Next Generation Standards." Position statement. Arlington, VA: NSTA. www.nsta.org/about/contact.aspx.

Reeves, D. 2002. *Making Standards Work: How to Implement Standards-Based Assessments in the Classroom, School, and District*. 3rd ed. Denver, CO: Advanced Learning Press.

Rivkin, M.S. 2014. *The Great Outdoors: Advocating for Natural Spaces for Young Children*. Rev. ed. Washington, DC: NAEYC.

About the Authors

Gera Jacobs, EdD, is a professor of early childhood education at the University of South Dakota. She served as president of the National Association for the Education of Young Children from 2012 to 2014. Gera is the author of articles that have published in national and regional journals and is the coauthor of several books for educators.

Kathy Crowley is a kindergarten teacher, and she has taught preschool through the primary grades. Kathy is the coauthor of several books for educators. The National Catholic Education Association presented her the Lead. Learn. Proclaim. Award in 2016.

The Importance of Deep Thought in Mathematics Interactions: Why Focusing on the Answer Is Not the Answer

Eugene A. Geist

"All right," said Deep Thought. "The Answer to the Great Question . . ."

"Yes . . . !"

"Of Life, the Universe and Everything . . ." said Deep Thought.

"Yes . . ."

"Is . . ." said Deep Thought, and paused.

"Yes . . . !"

"Is . . ."

"Yes . . . !!! . . . ?"

"Forty-two," said Deep Thought, with infinite majesty and calm.

"Forty-two!" yelled Loonquawl. "Is that all you've got to show for seven and a half million years' work?"

"I checked it very thoroughly," said the computer, "and that quite definitely is the answer. I think the problem, to be quite honest with you, is that you've never actually known what the question is."

—Douglas Adams, *The Hitchhiker's Guide to the Galaxy*

Deep Thought's observation of Loonquawl has an interesting application to primary mathematics instruction. Many primary teachers focus so much on students obtaining the correct answers to math problems that they can lose track of the most important (and interesting) aspects of the learning process: the questions that arise in mathematics, and the thought processes children use to investigate those questions.

Mathematics, the "Correct" Answer Approach

In many primary classrooms, children have often spent a good deal of time answering lots of math problems as quickly as possible. Too often these answers require little or no deep thought to produce. They typically require children only to follow a sequence of steps that have been taught to them to get a "correct" answer as fast as possible. "Incorrect" answers are seen as a symptom of not following the set of steps taught appropriately. Sometimes even correct answers that do not follow the steps are considered incorrect. Sometimes children are penalized for not showing their work or claiming that they did the work in their head. This approach focuses on teaching children a limited number of ways to get the correct answer (e.g., the standard algorithm) and ensuring that children follow the steps precisely (Mulligan et al. 2015; Schwartz 2015). Feedback on the child's answer is usually limited to a red mark if the answer was incorrect and a grade on the paper.

This model of teaching mathematics does not enable teachers to understand and value

Promoting Mathematical Fluency

Many mathematics programs require children to answer many questions to promote mathematical fluency (Geist 2010). There is growing evidence that an overemphasis on speed and the implementation of timed tests, which require children to produce correct answers as quickly as possible, can be detrimental to the mathematics learning process and may even produce mathematics anxiety (Boaler 2014; Geist 2010). While being able to quickly, efficiently, and accurately recall basic mathematical computations and apply procedures to problems is an important goal for any mathematics program, there are many ways to achieve this other than requiring children to do as many problems as they can as fast as possible.

Fosnot and Dolk (2001) and Rosales (2015) suggest a process that they refer to as *mathematizing*. This process encourages fluency by engaging children in mathematical problems in the world around them. For example, when children play a card game such as Double War, they naturally use various math skills and computations, and they are motivated to do so as fast as possible to keep the game from getting boring.

In Double War a deck of cards is evenly split between two players. Each player turns over two cards, and the player with the highest sum of both sets of cards takes the cards. This process repeats until one or both players are out of cards, at which point the player(s) turn over the pile of cards they have collected by winning and use that pile of cards to continue the game. This game promotes fluency and mathematizing in many ways. First, the children enjoy the game so they are motivated to use mathematics. Second, on each turn each child has to add not only her own two cards to get a sum but also her opponent's cards in order to compare the two sums and determine which is greater. Third, if there are any disagreements as to who won the round, they discuss and argue until they come up with a solution that is acceptable to both players. Finally, the children have internal motivation to do these tasks as fast as possible—partly because of competition, but partly because they want to keep the game moving along so it does not become tedious. Such games are in stark contrast to timed tests, which have caused much anxiety for many students of mathematics over the years (Geist 2015).

children's thought processes. Examining the way a child thinks about and approaches a math problem offers a window into his mathematical world that simple test scores do not provide. For example, one second grade child received a low score on a math test of money concepts. Although he understood the concepts of addition and subtraction, he had simply mistaken nickels for quarters. It appeared that the teacher had not actually examined the errors in depth. The child had actually done more complicated computations than required because of the error, but he had received no acknowledgement for this work. By not accepting the child's minor mistake in visual recognition, the teacher had missed an opportunity to value his mathematical deep thinking and build his confidence in his math skills, and possibly developed an inaccurate view of the child's skills.

For many reasons—including the stresses of standardized testing—teachers often do not feel they have the time to develop their students' ability to think deeply about questions in mathematics. The pressures to prepare children for a test or for the next level of instruction can lead to an overemphasis on getting the correct answers instead of listening to children's often wonderful explanations of their thought processes and encouraging them to work out strategies for themselves. Many classroom mathematics programs, textbooks, and worksheets focus on teaching children specific methods of solving a problem and then giving them repeated practice using that method to get the answer (Geist 2010). Even though the Common Core State Standards (CCSS) encourage children to use their own methodologies, many teachers, worksheets, and textbooks still emphasize teaching a child how to solve the problem rather than allowing children to think deeply.

A Shift in Thinking About Mathematics

Given the importance of encouraging children's deep thinking in mathematics, how can teachers shift the focus of early mathematics from one that emphasizes correct answers to one that focuses on deep thinking? What if the standard model of mathematics instruction was replaced by one designed around the way Sir Andrew Wiles, a professor at the University of Oxford, approaches math? This is how Wiles talks about mathematics:

> Perhaps I can best describe my experience of doing mathematics in terms of a journey through a dark unexplored mansion. You enter the first room of the mansion and it's completely dark. You stumble around bumping into the furniture, but gradually you learn where each piece of furniture is. Finally, after six months or so, you find the light switch, you turn it on, and suddenly it's all illuminated. You can see exactly where you were. Then you move into the next room and spend another six months in the dark. So each of these breakthroughs, while sometimes they're momentary, sometimes over a period of a day or two, they are the culmination of—and couldn't exist without—the many months of stumbling around in the dark that proceed them. (PBS Online 2000)

Wiles famously solved a 350-year-old problem posed by lawyer and amateur mathematician Pierre de Fermat. He became intrigued by this problem at an early age:

> I grew up in Cambridge in England, and my love of mathematics dates from those early childhood days. . . . The best problem I ever found was in my local public library. This one book was all about one particular problem—Fermat's Last Theorem. This problem had been unsolved by mathematicians for 300 years. It looked so simple, and yet all the great mathematicians in history couldn't solve it. Here was a problem, that I, a 10-year-

old, could understand, and I knew from that moment that I would never let it go. I had to solve it. (PBS Online 2000)

After years of intensive work, Wiles later found a solution to that problem that had stumped mathematicians for centuries. It was the question that excited and intrigued Wiles, not the instant access to an answer. There were no set procedures for him to follow to solve the problem, because no one had solved it before (except maybe Fermat himself, although it's not clear that he did). Our goal in primary classrooms should be to foster a love of mathematics in children and an excitement for solving problems so that they grow up to feel a similar way about mathematics.

Common Core Mathematics Standards and Deep Thinking

The CCSS, although sometimes perceived to be the cause of many current problems in mathematics instruction, actually place a strong emphasis on encouraging children to explain mathematical strategies. In fact, the first standard for Mathematical Practice, applicable across grades, states this:

> **CCSS.MATH.PRACTICE.MP1: Make sense of problems and persevere in solving them.** Mathematically proficient students start by explaining to themselves the meaning of a problem and looking for entry points to its solution. They analyze givens, constraints, relationships, and goals. They make conjectures about the form and meaning of the solution and plan a solution pathway rather than simply jumping into a solution attempt. . . . (NGA & CCSSO 2010)

This is very different from a traditional approach of teaching a problem–solution methodology and then requiring students to repeat the process on numerous practice problems. Mathematical Practice standard 3 also makes clear that students should be expected to explain and defend their processes to their peers:

> **CCSS.MATH.PRACTICE.MP3 Construct viable arguments and critique the reasoning of others.** Mathematically proficient students understand and use stated assumptions, definitions, and previously established results in constructing arguments. They make conjectures and build a logical progression of statements to explore the truth of their conjectures. They are able to analyze situations by breaking them into cases, and can recognize and use counterexamples. They justify their conclusions, communicate them to others, and respond to the arguments of others. . . . (NGA & CCSSO 2010)

These standards are based on what we know about the way children develop mathematical thinking. However, encouraging children to think deeply and meaningfully about mathematics requires a fundamental shift in the way educators teach mathematics to children in the primary grades. So how can you support children's problem solving and the process of thinking mathematically? This article lays out three steps: First, focus on the child's deep thinking rather than on correct answers. Second, allow children to use their own natural thinking ability to come up with as many ways as possible to solve a problem instead of teaching them just one. And finally, encourage children to talk, discuss, share, and argue their answers with their peers.

Deep Thinking

Deep mathematical thinking is better supported through inquiry activities, projects, discussion and argument, and games than through workbook pages and worksheets. Teachers can use project-based curricula to help children use mathematics to analyze, model, and solve real-world problems. Games and mathematical puzzles, such as the Double War game mentioned in the box on page 56, can be added to learning centers for children to explore on their own or in small groups without teacher supervision. When teachers encourage children's thinking, creative problem solving, and articulation of their ideas, they often see the result—a deep conceptual understanding in children.

Here is a transcript of a discussion with a first-grader and his parents, initiated by the child during dinner.

> Child: Did you know that 100 plus 100 is two?
>
> Adult 1: I want you to explain to me why 100 plus 100 is . . . what?
>
> Child: Two!
>
> Adult 1: Why is that?
>
> Child: Because . . . because zero and zero is nothing!
>
> Adult 1: Ok, and where did you get the two from?
>
> Child: Ummmm . . . ummmm . . . ummm. Me! (laughs)
>
> Adult 1: What equals two?
>
> Adult 2: How did you get two?
>
> Child: Ummm . . . two plus two is four.
>
> Adult 1: Yeah? So why is 100 plus 100 two?
>
> Child: (becoming agitated) Because zero plus zero is NOTHING!

Adult 1: Okay. Then where is the two? Where does the two come from?

Child: Um, from the one and one.

Adult 1: Okay, thank you.

This is an example of a child with a wrong answer but with some impressive conceptual knowledge. He had previously been able to give the correct answer to 100 plus 100 with little effort, but had recently learned the concept that 0 plus 0 was nothing. So he took this new knowledge and applied it to what he already knew. This process created a riddle in his mind that he found interesting: "How can 100 plus 100 be 200 if 0 plus 0 is nothing?" It was so intriguing to him that he shared it with his family.

It is important to notice that at no time during the discussion did either adult try to correct him or tell him that he was wrong. The focus was on the deep thought that the child had put into this explanation. The adults did not correct the child's wrong answer, but neither did they tell him that he was correct. Their goal was to elicit the child's explanation for *how* he got his answer. By doing this, the adults were able to see that the child was playing with the concept of addition using zero and place value. To tell the child that he was wrong would have halted this creative and inventive thought process—and possibly discouraged further wrestling with the concepts involved. Instead, the adults focused on the concepts and used questioning to help the child share his creative thinking.

While it can be very difficult to refrain from telling children that their answer is correct or incorrect or suggesting where the error lies, it is more beneficial that children be encouraged to find these errors and misconceptions for themselves. Giving the child an answer stops the thinking process. Teachers (and parents) need to find ways to extend the process, not end it. Instead, adults should ask questions like "How do you know that?" or even something more complex, such as "Well, if 100 and 100 is two, what is 50 and 50?" The child might apply the same reasoning and answer that 50 and 50 is 10.

Focusing on a correct answer is a linear process that goes from problem to solution (see Fig. 1). Deep thinking, in contrast, is a circular process of ever-increasing complexity (see Fig. 2). In the situation above, over the few weeks that followed the dinner discussion, the child's parents talked to him about other problems that included the addition of zero and also problems that required some place value knowledge. The following conversation occurred while the child and his father went to get ice cream.

A: So, Michael, if I have two 10-dollar bills in my pocket, how much money do I have?

C: 20!

A: How do you know?

C: Because 10 plus 10 is 20.

A: But I thought that the zeros added up to nothing.

C: Ohhh, yeeeahhh. I forgot about that. So you have two dollars [laughs].

A: Oh well, I guess I don't have enough money to get ice cream, then. Let's just go home.

C: NOOO! I know you have 20 dollars! Because you have two 10s, and 10 and 10 is 20!

A: Are you sure? I don't want to be short when I get there.

C: I am REALLY, REALLY sure!

Again the adult does not correct the child or tell him that he is right; he simply asks the child if he is sure about his answer. This encourages the circular process of deep thought. When a teacher tells a child that he is correct or incorrect, all thought on that problem stops, as shown in Figure 1. However, if a teacher simply asks, "How do you know that?" or encourages children to discuss their answers with others, the cycle in Figure 2 takes place. This type of math talk and discussion between people is one of the most significant ways to promote deep thinking in children, and it is what Mathematical Practice standards 1 and 3 of the Common Core Mathematics Standards promote.

Figure 1. The "correct" answer approach

Question → Answer → Correct? — Yes / No

Figure 2. Cycle of deep thought

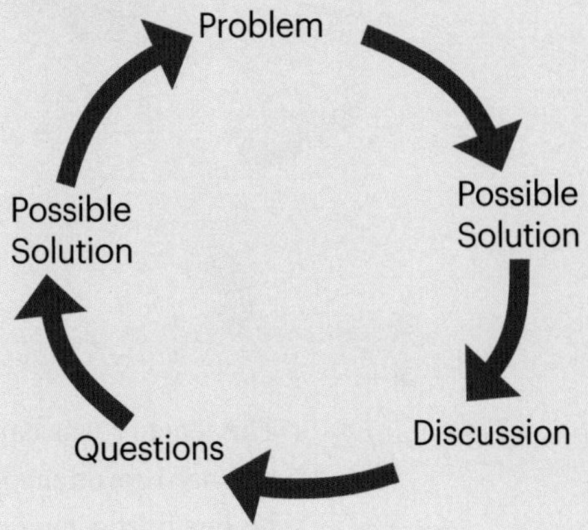

Problem → Possible Solution → Discussion → Questions → Possible Solution → Problem

Many Roads: Same Destination

To promote deep thinking in the classroom, the goal should be to create a safe place for children to play with ideas—to ponder, deliberate, make connections—about mathematics without being penalized for getting an incorrect answer.

This type of mathematical learning requires an emphasis on the process of solving problems rather than the answer. This may seem contradictory. You may wonder, "How can children learn mathematics if I don't tell them what they did wrong?" The answer is that through discussion children reexamine their processes and also learn how others approached the problem. As the children listen and think and try to understand other children's processes, they will in turn examine their own. Here is an example from a first grade classroom. The teacher wrote the problem *25 + 35* on the board and then gave children time to think about the answer.

Teacher: Amber, tell us how you got your answer.

Amber: I took the 20 and the 30 and knew that that was 50 and then I knew 5 plus 5 more was 10, so I added 10 more on to get 60.

Teacher: [writing this process on the chalkboard] So you knew 20 plus 30 equaled 50 and five and five was 10 more. So then you did 50 plus 10 and that equaled 60.

Millie: I got 60, but I did it differently.

Teacher: Okay, Millie, how did you do it?

Millie: I took 5 off of 25 and put it on the 35 and that made 40.

Teacher: [writing this process on the chalkboard] Okay.

Millie: Then I knew that 40 plus 20 was 60 and that was my answer!

The teacher was careful not to tell each child if she was correct or incorrect. Instead the teacher reproduced the children's thinking on the chalkboard for all to see. In this case no one in the class disagreed with Amber's answer, but Millie did point out another way of solving the problem, so the teacher encouraged Millie to explain her method to the class also. When children are encouraged to come up with their own methods for solving problems and consider their peers' explanations of other strategies, they build a conceptual knowledge of mathematics that they cannot gain through rote memorization of math facts (Kamii & Joseph 2004).

The teacher also did not present a lesson on how to solve problems that require regrouping, as is the standard practice before presenting children with a problem like this one. Usually the teacher would show the children how to add the two 5s in the ones column and then carry over 10 to the tens column. However, in this example the teacher let the children construct their own ways of solving the problem. Although neither child used the standard algorithm to solve the problem, the methodologies they used were derived from their existing understanding of mathematics. One child knew that 5 plus 5 was 10, and the other knew that 25 minus 5 was 20 and 35 plus 5 was 40. They used what they knew to solve the problem.

If you notice that some children are using regrouping in their solutions, as often happens, you could point this out and tell the class that this is called *regrouping* and it can be helpful in solving large addition problems. Then the students could choose to use it if they wished or they could use a different method that worked better for them. For example, regrouping works well for me when I am using a pencil and paper to add large numbers, but I have difficulty using regrouping as a mental strategy for solving problems when I have nothing to write on. When I try, I end up using my finger to draw invisible numbers in the air. Likewise, children should be encouraged to decide when to use which strategy. Teaching just one strategy, such as regrouping, limits the ability of children to think deeply about a problem.

Arguing for Understanding

Many adults will recognize from their own mathematics education the typical sequence of events that occur when teachers present a math problem (see Fig. 3). Figure 3 shows the way many class discussions are traditionally conducted, with teachers posing the question and then informing children if they are correct or incorrect. With this method, teachers cannot examine children's thought processes. It sends the message to children that there is only one way to solve a particular problem and that the teacher is the final authority when it comes to the answer. For many students, this method may lead to a lifetime dislike of mathematics and even math phobias (Boaler 2014; Geist 2010).

However, with some simple adjustments to the way a teacher responds to children's answers, classroom discussions can support children's deep thinking about the problem and construction of mathematical knowledge. As Figure 4 on the next page illustrates, the teacher does not tell the child if the answer she gives is correct or incorrect. Instead, all children are asked if they agree with the answer. If not, then discussion and argument are used to convince others of the merits of the solution—and of other solutions put forth—and to find any flaws in the method used to get to the answer.

When children have to defend their answer to others, they must fully understand it themselves and construct arguments to support their solution, clearly presenting their logic in ways that are readily understandable by others. This ability is also recognized in the Common Core State Standards, as mentioned previously. Many times this process leads children to recognize a flaw in their own thinking (Kamii & Joseph 2004).

A second grade teacher, a bit doubtful about not telling children the answers, nonetheless gave this approach a try. When one of her students answered a problem incorrectly during a class discussion, instead of pointing out her error, the teacher held out the chalk to the student and asked her to show the class how she got her answer. As the child stood and reached out to take the chalk she suddenly said, "Oh! No, I think I made a mistake! I think I am wrong!" and sat down again. The teacher then asked her to show the class her new solution. As she did, the child explained that she had recognized her error when she was visualizing how to prove to everyone that her original answer was correct.

Figure 4 illustrates a more complex approach to facilitating discussion about a mathematics problem. The first four steps are the same, but at the first fork in the model the *children* are asked to give input on the answers, not the teacher. The process is driven by the children's discussion of their answers and their solutions. The teacher's role is not to tell them who is correct and incorrect, but to encourage children to think through the problem and its possible solutions. Students are encouraged to talk to each other and even be passionate

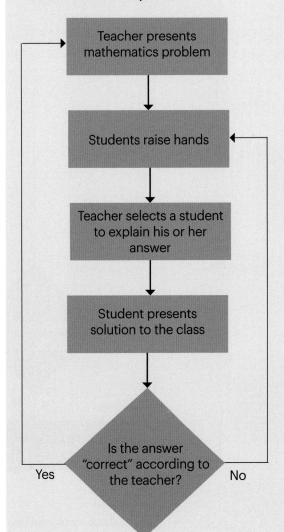

Figure 3. Process leading to the "correct" answer to a problem

Teacher presents mathematics problem

Students raise hands

Teacher selects a student to explain his or her answer

Student presents solution to the class

Is the answer "correct" according to the teacher?

Yes   No

Figure 4. Process supporting deep thinking about a problem

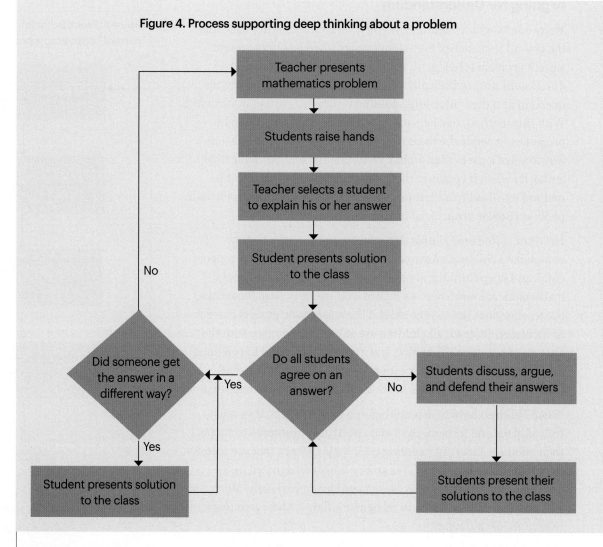

about their solutions. Most important, children are encouraged to stick with their answer until they are convinced that someone else has a better answer (Kamii & Joseph 2004). The teacher's job becomes one of facilitator and moderator rather than one of judge and jury.

A wonderful video of a first grade class working on a mathematics problem offers a great example of this approach (Kamii & Clark 2000). The problem was "Joe has 62 cents and erasers cost 5 cents at the school store. How many erasers can Joe buy?" The teacher asked a student sitting at a table with two other students to explain her answer. The child said that she counted by 5s and wrote it down on her paper. On her paper she had written the numbers *5, 10, 15, 20, 25, 30, 35, 40, 45, 50, 55, 60,* and *62.* Underneath she had written a big *13* and circled it. The student explained that she had counted all the numbers and got 13. The student to her left said that he disagreed with her answer. The teacher, instead of telling them which child was correct, said, "Why do you think that?" The other student said he didn't know what she had done wrong, but that he had gotten an answer of 12 and that she must have counted wrong. The girl defended her answer, saying that she had done exactly what the boy had done but had arrived at an answer of 13. And she ran through her process again, sticking to her answer until she finally saw and understood her error. This took a few minutes of back-and-forth discussion, but all through it the teacher encouraged both children to explain their points of view. When the girl finally saw her mistake and corrected her answer, the teacher asked her if she was sure and then moved on to another student.

But what if at the end of the lesson there are still disagreements? In that case, students can be asked to think about the problem at home and discuss it with their family members. In a way, it is much like Andrew Wiles and Fermat's theorem in that these students are developing proofs to support their answers and then explaining them in a way to convince others that their solution is correct.

Conclusion

Teaching students to develop fluency and work at a reasonable pace is something that is achieved through the careful development of numerical understanding in the early years of school. Learning is a process that takes time, and it cannot be accelerated by methods that encourage speed at the expense of understanding. (Boaler 2014, 469)

Deep thinking about mathematics allows children to value the process of solving problems and see the merit of using many different ways to solve problems. Children have a natural curiosity and drive to understand their world, and mathematics is a vital tool in that process. The more mathematical tools they have available to them, the deeper they can think about the world around then. This can also foster a love of mathematics instead of anxiety. By promoting deep thought and problem solving in the primary grades instead of emphasizing correct answers, teachers help children see how vital mathematics is to their lives. If we want to foster a love of reading in children, we give them interesting books and stories to read that relate to their lives. If we want to foster a love of mathematics, we need to give children interesting problems to solve that relate to their lives. This will help to prepare children for math tests and, more importantly, prepare them for a lifetime of mathematical reasoning.

Making changes like these in the classroom takes careful planning. Communicating and working with families is vitally important to this type of teaching. Many parents will have learned mathematics in a very different, more traditional way, and may not be clear on how their children are actually learning with these "new" methods. They might be confused by some of the wild and creative ways their children come up with to solve problems. However, simple, reassuring communication and encouragement for them to listen to their children's explanations, hold back on correcting their errors, and value their thinking can help parents to understand the importance of promoting deep mathematical thinking.

Having children involve their family members in mathematical discussions can help too. Send home brain teasers that have several different answers or many different ways to arrive at an answer. Families can discuss them at mealtime or in the car. Emphasize to families that talking to children about mathematics is as important as reading to them and that math talk can be a part of their everyday routines—money, time, cooking, measurement, or any other activity where mathematics is used.

Deep thinking about mathematics in the primary grades has numerous payoffs. Children are less likely to develop math anxiety, they have a deeper conceptual understanding of mathematics, and they may develop a lifelong affinity for mathematics much as Andrew Wiles has (Boaler 2014). They may not all become mathematicians, but they will always retain the ability to think like one.

References

Boaler, J. 2014. "Research Suggests That Timed Tests Cause Math Anxiety." *Teaching Children Mathematics* 20 (8): 469–74.

Fosnot, C.T., & M. Dolk. 2001. *Young Mathematicians at Work: Constructing Multiplication and Division.* Portsmouth, NH: Heinemann.

Geist, E. 2010. "The Anti-Anxiety Curriculum: Combating Math Anxiety in the Classroom." *Journal of Instructional Psychology* 37 (1): 24–31.

Geist, E. 2015. "Math Anxiety and the 'Math Gap': How Attitudes Toward Mathematics Disadvantages Students as Early as Preschool." *Education* 135 (3): 328–36.

Kamii, C., & F.C. Clark. 2000. *First Graders Dividing 62 by 5: A Teacher Uses Piaget's Theory.* Video. New York: Teachers College Press.

Kamii, C., & L.L. Joseph. 2004. *Young Children Continue to Reinvent Arithmetic—2nd Grade: Implications of Piaget's Theory.* 2nd ed. New York: Teachers College Press.

Mulligan, G.M., J.C. McCarroll, K.D. Flanagan, & D. Potter. 2015. *Findings From the Second-Grade Rounds of the Early Childhood Longitudinal Study, Kindergarten Class of 2010–11 (ECLS-K:2011): First Look.* NCES 2015-077. Washington, DC: National Center for Education Statistics. http://nces.ed.gov/pubs2015/2015077.pdf.

NGA (National Governors Association) & CCSSO (Council of Chief State School Officers). 2010. "Standards for Mathematical Practice." www.corestandards.org/Math/Practice.

PBS Online. 2000. "Andrew Wiles on Solving Fermat." http://nova.wgbhdigital.org/wgbh/nova/physics/andrew-wiles-fermat.html.

Rosales, A.C. 2015. *Mathematizing: An Emergent Math Curriculum Approach for Young Children.* St. Paul, MN: Redleaf.

Schwartz, C. 2015. "Developing the Practice of Teacher Questioning Through a K–2 Elementary Mathematics Field Experience." *Investigations in Mathematics Learning* 7 (3): 30–50.

About the Author

Eugene Geist, PhD, is associate professor in the Patton College of Education at Ohio University. He has teaching responsibilities in the Early Childhood Education program, the Connavino Honors Program, and the Curriculum and Instruction doctoral program. His areas of expertise include child development, constructivism, and the development of mathematical knowledge in young children.

Investigating the Role of Interactive Technology in a First Grade Classroom

Charity-Ann J. Baker

igital technology is a signature of our times, yet questions remain about how teachers can best engage young children with related tools. To explore and document how the first-graders I teach respond to the interactive technology, tools, and software in my classroom, I decided to investigate the following questions:

> When used effectively, how do interactive technologies—including digital whiteboards, document cameras, computers, and select software resources—impact the young learners in my classroom?

> Are these technological tools developmentally appropriate for early childhood students?

Literature Review

Young children are active learners, and the new set of digital tools called *interactive technology*—defined as any technological hardware device or software that one actively engages with through voice, sound, touch, or other means of sensory involvement—can meet the needs of active learners. Puerling's *Teaching in the Digital Age* (2012) was critical in shifting my mindset from classroom technology use in general to focusing on interactive technology's impact on young learners. He suggests that these new technologies can enhance the way both teachers and children gather, share, analyze, and apply information.

Most children ages 6–9 are exposed to or interact with multiple forms of media and devices daily. Early childhood educators have the opportunity to take that foundational exposure and use it to capitalize on children's strengths and improve weaknesses in a variety of cross-curricular and cross-modality areas (NAEYC & Fred Rogers Center 2012; Puerling 2012). To effectively employ new technologies as classroom tools and resources, teachers must stay current with technological standards and incorporate them into daily planning, instruction, and assessment. One such standard is the joint position statement on technology and interactive media issued by NAEYC and the Fred Rogers Center for Early Learning and Children's Media at Saint Vincent College, which affirms the potential benefits of technology for young children when integrated into developmentally appropriate practice:

> When the integration of technology and interactive media in early childhood programs is built upon solid developmental foundations, and early childhood professionals are aware of both the challenges and the opportunities, educators are positioned to improve program quality by intentionally leveraging the potential of technology and media for the benefit of every child. (NAEYC & Fred Rogers Center 2012)

Developmentally appropriate use of interactive media offers children access to a greater breadth and depth of learning. A child's cognitive capacity can be viewed narrowly as the ability to master specific skills, such as counting, identifying shapes, and matching appropriate letters and sounds. However, cognitive development is much broader than this. As students explore, investigate, and test out their ideas, they make connections, solve problems, draw conclusions, and make sense of the world around them (Wright & Shade 1994). Interactive technology can offer the support and opportunities for children to develop skills in using these critical cognitive strategies.

In addition, interactive technology meshes well with several learning characteristics of first-graders. For example, children this age

> Are increasingly interested in computers

> Learn best through discovery

> Love asking questions and trying out new games and ideas

> Enjoy the process more than the product

> Are beginning to be interested in skill and technique for their own sake (Wood 2007, 79)

These characteristics are highlighted in my classroom research and exemplify just how exciting the integration of interactive technology can be for first-graders.

Because a frequent critique of technology is that it isolates children from one another, peer interactions were important to my research—children interacting and learning through observation and imitation of one another, with more advanced peers serving as experts. When technology is used in collaborative, constructivist arrangements where the teacher is not the sole source of information, children develop skills both independently and with peers. Montessori consistently demonstrated how important it is that students are active participants in their learning; when teachers can begin to gradually release responsibility to children, providing them with the appropriate knowledge and tools to be successful, children's experiences inform their learning beyond the primary classroom (Mooney 2013).

I believe in constructivism and drew from Vygotsky's (1978) developmental theories on learning to frame my own and the children's interactions with each other as they used the technology. The constructivist perspective highlights that learning takes place during collaborative social interactions in a zone of proximal development; if a child cannot yet accomplish a task alone, she may be able to accomplish it with the help of an adult or a peer who has already mastered the task.

Methodology/Research Design

I conducted my research over the course of four months, from September to January. The 18 first grade children involved were from a variety of academic, linguistic, cultural, and socioeconomic backgrounds. They included children with learning disabilities and language acquisition difficulties or delays, and children from culturally underrepresented groups. At the start of the school year, I implemented a variety of new interactive technological and digital resources into planning and instruction. Hardware devices included an interactive whiteboard, a document camera, and six classroom computers. Software resources included educational websites such as Raz-Kids (an online guided reading program with interactive and downloadable ebooks), Starfall (phonics instruction incorporated into games and interactive ebooks), and The National Library of Virtual Manipulatives (a digital library containing interactive web-based mathematics activities for K–12), as well as word processing (Microsoft Word) and presentation programs (Microsoft PowerPoint, Prezi, and iMovie).

I collected data through

1. Observation of children's engagement and attitudes

2. Interviews with the children

3. Assessment of feelings about technology using happy/sad faces

4. Parent surveys

5. Investigation of children's academic progress through both online and traditional assessment measures

Observation of Engagement and Attitudes

I randomly placed the children in groups of six and assigned them tasks to complete independently at a computer. I kept tallies to note indications of disengagement (e.g., looking around the room) and appeals for adult help after my initial instructions and discussion. I kept anecdotal records on collaborative conversations among children during group work with the technology. This data helped me gauge children's confidence levels navigating various websites independently and gave me a clearer picture of their active interest.

Interactive Interviews

Interactive technology use is personal, and I wanted to learn about the children's experiences not only through my observations but also by asking them to communicate their feelings in their own words. Once a week I interviewed the children during our weekly one-on-one conferences. Sample questions included these:

> What is your favorite piece of technology in our classroom? Why?

> Who is the leader when you and your classmates work with technology?

> Are you good at using the technology in our classroom?

> Do you ever talk to your family members or friends about the technology in our classroom? Why or why not?

Later, I coded and analyzed the responses to uncover both positive and negative trends.

Assessment of Feelings About Technology

Students were asked to respond to the prompt "How does working with technology make you feel? Circle the face and words that show your feelings."

Parent Surveys

To understand how parents perceived children's use of technology in school and at home, I distributed a survey once a month to the parents or guardians of each child. They could complete the survey on paper or online. There were five questions geared toward parents' perceptions of their child's proficiency and attitudes regarding technology based on home conversations. The survey included these questions:

> How frequently does your child talk to you about the technology used in class?

> Do his or her reactions seem positive or negative to you?

> Explain what you think makes you feel he or she has a negative or positive attitude regarding technology.

> What particular programs, if any, have come up in conversation at home? Mark all [from a list of programs] that apply.

> What type of technology, if any, do you have at home that your son or daughter may be exposed to?

Investigations of Academic Progress

I felt it was important to collect data that could shed light on whether the skills and understandings the students constructed in the online programs contributed to their performance in offline classwork. I compared the children's performance on specific skills in the online literacy and math programs with the formal assessments of these skills. The assessments included monthly topic tests from the Growing With Mathematics Program, the Developmental Reading Assessment (DRA2), a phonological awareness assessment, a high-frequency word assessment, and a Words Their Way spelling inventory. For example, if a child moved forward in an online reading program, did she progress on formal assessments as well? Did children's success in the online programs relate to improved decoding accuracy, fluency, comprehension, number sense, and probability mastery in daily lessons? I analyzed my data by noting whether there was an alignment between online and offline tasks of mastery in these areas, coding positive versus negative trends.

Findings and Discussion

The interactive technology enriched the children's academic learning experiences and their peer interactions. It contributed to their cognitive and social competence in ways that were developmentally appropriate for young learners. In my research, six major findings surfaced:

> Children took on cognitive challenges and applied online learning to offline tasks and vice versa, integrating the two.

> Children gained confidence in their use of technology, which fostered higher levels of self-esteem and independence, prompting more active roles in their learning and ownership of their work.

> Children's oral and written communication skills improved.

> The traditional roles of teacher and child were altered; as children gradually took more responsibility for their learning and became more self-directed, I became a facilitator of their learning.

> Children engaged in more collaborative interactions with each other.

> Children were more apt to communicate about their learning outside of school.

Integrated Online and Offline Learning

The software and online programs provided children with a variety of tools, rather than a fixed set of options, to explore ideas. These tools were designed to foster children's

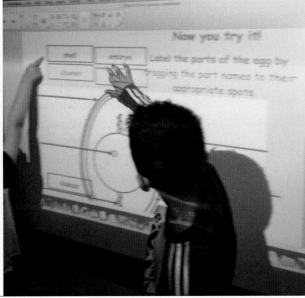

problem solving and critical thinking, such as discovering the interaction between things or seeing the predictability of cause-and-effect relationships (Wright & Shade 1994). The children willingly took on these challenges, which required them to find solutions to content problems as well as to technical issues. Multimedia programs like Raz-Kids, Starfall, and RoytheZebra worked within children's zone of proximal development to help them move at their own pace and ability while at the same time providing challenge. Raz-Kids, specifically, supported their efforts by allowing the children to set higher-order tasks as long-term goals, all the while motivating them to learn the lower-level skills needed to get there.

The children applied the strategies they learned through their use of the interactive technology to their offline work in the same subject area and began to make connections between their online and offline learning. For example, when asked how technology helps him with his favorite subject, a child explained, "You learn how to read because I see the words on the SMART Board from the document camera and then the same words in my book and they're snap [sight] words because I've seen them before!" This student recognized that the words he saw on the SMART Board were the same words that he saw in other texts, and he demonstrated an understanding of how this learning nests in a broader, more global context as a reader.

As highlighted in this anecdote, the use of technology seemed to increase the children's ability to self-monitor for problem solving. Children recognized that they were confused or needed to make changes, especially when they came to reading tricky words in online passages. This child was clearly self-monitoring his reading, and his ability to recognize familiar print with ease fostered more fluent reading overall. When asked which technology is most helpful, children identified their ability to read books on the computer, watch strategies modeled on the document camera, and type their own stories.

The children not only used the technology tools to supplement their traditional forms of learning, they also incorporated their offline learning strategies into their work in the same subject areas online as it became woven into the everyday curriculum. For example, in the bookrooms in Raz-Kids, children used their repertoire of decoding and comprehension strategies learned in class to accurately decode and comprehend (in both literal and evaluative ways) the various fiction and nonfiction texts.

Through my academic assessments, I found a close alignment between the areas that were most covered in the online literacy and math programs and the areas of most academic improvement as measured by formal assessment tools. This suggested that the children were applying their online learning and that a beneficial relationship existed between online and offline learning. For example, children whose decoding and comprehension skills increased on Raz-Kids showed similar improvement in these areas on the Developmental Reading Assessment. Similarly, children who successfully completed lessons from The National Library of Virtual Manipulatives website (on number concepts, operations of addition and subtraction, patterning, and measurement of time, length, and money) showed dramatic increases in corresponding areas on formal mathematics assessments.

Active Roles in Learning and Ownership of Work

Children were naturally motivated by the interactive aspect of technology in the classroom. As they used it more frequently, they became more familiar with it. Ultimately, familiarity bred confidence, and confidence created a catalyst for independence. This in turn led to more active roles in their learning and ownership of their work.

The children enjoyed using the technology and became more confident using classroom computers—and more confident in technology use overall. When asked near the end of the study, "Are you good at using technology?," all 18 students answered yes. The children explained that they knew a lot about technology for various reasons. For example, one child said, "When you try, you realize you know how to do something." As this quote illustrates, the children were beginning to take risks as their confidence with classroom technology grew—they were able to discover their strengths at a personally relevant pace. Many even went on to describe how they used it at home and helped their parents as well.

The number of appeals for help from me decreased dramatically over the course of the study. By the end of the study, each child sustained attention and was able to navigate sites independently. When the children initiated and directed their own computer use, they felt they were being allowed to use a "grown-up" machine. In addition, greater legibility of typed pieces encouraged children to publically display their efforts, which provided more opportunities for positive feedback.

The interactive technology actively engaged the students, and their drive to participate meant they remained on task. All of the students responded "happy" or "very happy" in their ratings of technology use in the classroom. One child's view changed dramatically over the course of the study. In the first week of research, he responded that he was "very sad" about working with technology because "technology turns your brain to mush." This was a view his mother had shared with him, specifically referring to television use. But by the third week, this student began responding that he was "very happy" and eventually became excited to use the technology; he asked to use it often and laughed aloud when reading online literature. He said he hadn't realized that technology was all the "stuff" around him in school—he had just thought technology meant television. He remarked, "Technology is so much fun and it makes your brain bigger, too." This, he explained, was because you learn much more with technology than you would without it. This example provides a good illustration of the emotional involvement of the children with the technology and the enhanced self-understanding it gendered.

The children favored the active, participatory roles that interactive technology offered. When given the choice, children always chose to engage with interactive technology rather than watch brief educational videos covering the relevant concepts. They seemed to prefer taking an active role and deciding the next steps of an activity for themselves on a digital whiteboard over passively watching a video and having that decision made for them. As they used the interactive technology, the children were experiencing—actively participating in—their learning during every step of the study. For instance, the whiteboard enabled children to physically engage with concepts by touching the board and moving words around. The children could model an activity for classmates on the whiteboard via the document camera—zooming into a book, pointing to a specific spot in their writing, or working through a mathematics task. The classroom document camera also allowed me to represent ideas through the use of real objects, three-dimensional pictures, graphs, and physical models, which enhanced the students' experience and helped them better understand newly presented information.

Improved Oral and Written Communication Skills

The interactive nature of the technology helped support children's development of communication skills. Fluency, expression, grammar, and both oral and written activities were impacted. For example, the children performed their own digital stories using iMovie software, which allowed them to record their voices and act out the stories with facial expressions and gestures appropriate to their characters. Students then played back the recordings to self-monitor their speaking rate, expressions, and volume; based on this, sometimes they rerecorded their stories. (Digital storytelling is a brief, multimedia production that allows children to share personal narratives or informational pieces that include photographs, videos, sound, music, text, and most important, the storyteller's voice.)

A feature in Raz-Kids also enhanced oral communication skills by allowing children to use a Mac computer's built-in speaker to record their reading. Playing back the readings later, when I had more time to listen to their reading fluency and expressiveness, helped me assess their reading skills. Within the assessed passages, children demonstrated an increased number of self-corrections as well as improvements in general self-monitoring of rate, volume, and expression. This information was useful feedback for the children during my daily conferences with them.

In addition to oral language, interactive technology seemed to positively impact the children's written skills. Children used the computer to help communicate their thoughts and ideas and tell their story in print. My journal records indicated that using word processing programs resulted in writing that was stronger, more clearly organized, and more detailed. The programs also honed children's use of standard conventions of grammar and mechanics.

As my research proceeded, children were still required to complete written assignments in class using pencil and paper. During these instances, most children would skip words that were difficult to spell, ask me to spell words for them, or try to use easier synonyms (like *bad* instead of *horrible*). This impeded the flow of their writing and their willingness to take academic risks.

When they wrote on the computer, however, they recognized that they needed to make decisions about the appropriateness of a word underlined in red. As one child exclaimed, "I've got to figure out how to get rid of that red squiggly under my word—it's not spelled right!"

This did not mean that the children's writing was always free of spelling errors. However, because the technology highlighted spelling, mechanical, and grammatical errors, children had to sort through their resources to find the relevant solution and fix their mistakes independently.

Over time, revising their work for spelling errors led to the children revising their work in general. Before long, they were independently adding to and deleting words and sentences, and their pieces became more organized overall. With increased revision strategies, they began writing in a more focused way, targeting one particular topic or idea. This was a tremendous area of growth for students who, at the start of my research, included multiple, tangential ideas in a single piece.

Molly recommends a book series.

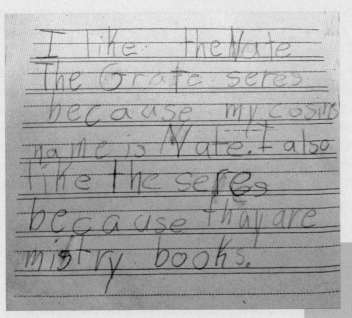

There are four reasons that I like the Nate the Great series. First I like the series because my cousin's name is Nate. I also like the series because they are mystery books and I like to read on to find out what is going to happen next. Then, I like Nate the Great because they are chapter books and have a lot of details. Finally, I like Nate the Great because the books have author's purpose. The books entertain a reader because they have details. I read six Nate the Great books and I like the series!

I like the Nate The Grate seres because my cosins name is Nate. I also like the seres because thay are mistry books.

It took children a bit more time to type rather than to write on paper because they were still familiarizing themselves with the keyboard. However, taking the extra time was worth it—as the children's skills grew, they began to elaborate on their ideas with more descriptive language (see the *Nate the Great* example on page 75). They added details and integrated techniques from our Writing Workshop mini-lessons, such as strong leads and transition words.

Children used the computer to help communicate their thoughts and ideas, and they genuinely enjoyed writing in a new way. They demonstrated high levels of interest in "publishing" books by typing stories and made frequent comments about "being real authors" because their writing looked more professional when printed. For young learners, this change made all the difference to the feeling of ownership and accountability they had over their work, and ultimately resulted in more refined pieces of writing.

Changing Roles

The interactive technology helped me focus more on placing the children at the center of attention. My findings concurred with a US Department of Education (2010) study that found that when children use technology, the teacher is no longer "the dispenser of information, but rather plays the role of facilitator." I began to see this change in roles right away. For example, when children manipulated objects on the document camera or participated in an activity on the whiteboard, they actively determined their own actions. They didn't depend solely on me for help and information.

Interactive, multimedia technology also allowed me to shift my instructional techniques to differentiate material more concretely. Young children need a lot of one-on-one attention, and interactive software helps with that. The programs contained a nearly inexhaustible pool of resources for discovery and allowed children of completely different ability levels to work alongside one another on tasks targeting their unique strengths. If I used technology effectively as a supplement to instruction, I was better able to facilitate learning and monitor a greater number of children. I was also more likely to conference individually with each child.

As the children's independence levels increased, so did mine. I had a greater ability, over time, to set project goals for children to work on independently, and I could move from child to child to tackle specific questions or challenges. Specifically, during our balanced literacy block, I increased the number of individual conferences from seven students to all 18 students by Week 4 of my study. I never got the impression that the children felt I was constantly looking over their shoulders—rather, they were excited to share the details of their progress with me when I conferenced with them. One conversation took place as follows:

> Charity: Take a look on the Bookmarks Tab for some kid-friendly sites to get started on your research about a frog's life cycle. I'll check back with you in a few minutes.
>
> (*Four minutes pass.*)
>
> Charity: How is it going with your frog research over here?
>
> Child: It's great! You'll never believe what I found, Mrs. Baker! Did you know that there is a stage where the frogs are called *froglets* between the time they're tadpoles and frogs?

Charity: Isn't that interesting? Excellent research. Be sure you write down what body parts grow during the froglet stage on your research sheet.

Child: Got it!

With me acting as a facilitator, children had the time and opportunity to share their learning and gain support and validation for their efforts.

More Collaborative Interactions

I partnered and grouped students with different academic abilities together. In my observations, when children completed a puzzle together or built with blocks with a partner or in small groups, there tended to be one main leader of communication. In contrast, the interactive technology I used invited children to share a leadership role. When children arrived at a computer or whiteboard together, they had to decide whose turn it was and resolve disagreements about the specific sequence of the activities. Once this process was learned (a significant social lesson in itself), I was able to guide the children toward finding solutions to the problem or activity collaboratively. Eventually, peer mentoring evolved and children excitedly became "teachers" for each other (Bruner, Caudill, & Ninio 1997). With some teacher guidance, the children gained new social skills as they eventually learned the difference between *completing* and *explaining* a program for a peer who needed assistance. The following are examples from my anecdotal records that show children mentoring and helping each other:

So, click there [pointing to the screen] and then see what happens.

Hey, I need a math mentor on this one. Can you help me?

When you get to a tricky word, you can click on it and it will tell you what it says. Here, watch me do it first, then you can try it. But you gotta make sure you have the headphones on to hear it, okay?

As students began to mentor each other, they reinforced newly learned concepts in a more mutual way. When I asked children, "Who is the 'leader' when you and your classmates work with technology?," a few attributed leadership to themselves or someone else ("Sometimes me or sometimes [name of partner]"; "You, Mrs. Baker. Of course you are!").

However, 13 of the 18 students expressed a much more collaborative tone:

> Both of us.
>
> I don't know, there's not supposed to be a leader.
>
> No one! 'Cause we're working together!

Over the course of the study, I noticed an increase in collaboration even when each student had access to an individual computer in a laboratory setting. In addition to our computers, the classroom document camera also sparked student collaboration. It allowed students to showcase demonstrations and model work for their peers on the whiteboard. After all, "Large screens offer a way to invite an audience into what is occurring on and in front of the screen" (Puerling 2012, 74).

When I asked the children how it felt to work with a partner, everyone responded positively (e.g., "Excited," "Super," "Fun! Really, really fun!"). They explained that they liked the experience because they could help each other. What makes employing interactive technology so different from any other child-centered classroom activity I've experienced is the symbiotic relationship of peers: There were consistently mutual benefits among the partnerships.

Communicating Learning Outside of School

Children's interest in multimedia technology didn't stop at the end of the school day; their use of the technology actually promoted educational conversation outside of school. Children not only talked more about technology as they became more familiar with it, they also shared more information about what the technology was helping them learn. As one parent shared in a weekly survey, "I noticed that [my child's] work with the classroom technology has definitely increased 'computer talk' between her and my husband. It also has made her share more [about school] during general 'school conversation' too." The parent explained that her child had visited a virtual museum on the whiteboard that day in class and voluntarily described her findings to family at home. This example reminded me of the importance of helping families better understand the benefits of technology for everyday learning. As Puerling (2012) states,

> Families want to support their children and often rely on teachers for insight on how to do this. . . . When you are confident in your practice and can clearly articulate how technology supports their children's growth and development, families are more likely to develop comfort and support for the technology's presence in the classroom. (212)

The parent surveys invited families into the conversation about our classroom technology and presented very positive feedback. The result was cyclical—when parents were aware of what their children were learning with technology and felt involved in this process, children seemed more enthusiastic to converse with them. When the children talked about technology use more frequently and with greater enthusiasm, families seemed to become more comfortable with children using it in the classroom. As parents reported, by the fourth and final month of the study, 16 of my 18 students had discussed our classroom technology at home at least once a day.

Conclusion

My research highlights how interactive multimedia (specifically, digital whiteboards, document cameras, and classroom computers) can be developmentally appropriate for young children, leading to greater collaboration and more participatory, active learning. I found that interactive technology contributed to improved literacy skills in reading and writing, which are especially critical in primary classrooms. Integration of technology, offered as a supplemental tool in the early childhood classroom, does not distance the teacher from instruction. As my research shows, it actually gave me more time for individual conferencing with children, moving them to a central place of focus in the classroom as constructors and owners of knowledge. I also found that rather than socially isolating children, technology use fostered more collaborative interactions with peers and enhanced parent understanding of children's learning at school.

References

Bruner, J.S., E. Caudill, & A. Ninio. 1997. "Language and Experience." In *John Dewey Reconsidered,* ed. R.S. Peters. London: Routledge & Kegan Paul.

Mooney, C.G. 2013. *Theories of Childhood: An Introduction to Dewey, Montessori, Erikson, Piaget, and Vygotsky.* 2nd ed. St. Paul, MN: Redleaf.

NAEYC & Fred Rogers Center. 2012. "Technology and Interactive Media as Tools in Early Childhood Programs Serving Children From Birth Through Age 8." Joint position statement. Washington, DC: NAEYC; Latrobe, PA: Fred Rogers Center for Early Learning and Children's Media at Saint Vincent College. www.naeyc.org/content/technology-and-young-children.

Puerling, B. 2012. *Teaching in the Digital Age: Smart Tools for Age 3 to Grade 3.* St. Paul, MN: Redleaf.

US Department of Education. 2010. "Effects of Technology on Classroom and Students." Washington, DC: US Department of Education. www2.ed.gov/pubs/EdReformStudies/EdTech/effectsstudents.html.

Vygotsky, L.S. 1978. *Mind in Society: The Development of Higher Psychological Processes.* Cambridge, MA: Harvard University Press.

Wood, C. 2007. *Yardsticks: Children in the Classroom, Ages 4–14.* 3rd ed. Turners Falls, MA: Northeast Foundation for Children.

Wright, J.L., & D.D. Shade, eds. 1994. *Young Children: Active Learners in a Technological Age.* Washington, DC: NAEYC.

About the Author

Charity-Ann J. Baker, EdS, is a teacher leader for Southington Public Schools, in Southington, Connecticut, and a part-time instructor for the University of Saint Joseph in West Hartford, Connecticut. Charity-Ann continually advocates for the primary classroom and strives to infuse her passion for interactive technology into both her teaching and learning experiences.

This article was originally published in *Voices of Practitioners,* NAEYC's online teacher research journal. In teacher research, teachers engage in the systematic study of their own practice. Because teachers are deeply involved in the daily lives of children and their families, their investigations and reflections provide a critical inside perspective on teaching and learning in classrooms.

Social Studies From Early Childhood Education to the World

Gayle Mindes

An important educational reform initiated in 2009 by the Council of Chief School Officers and the National Governors Association resulted in the creation of the Common Core State Standards (CCSS). The CCSS were developed because of the wide variation in the level of expectations for student achievement across the country. The results of this irregularity can be seen in statistics for adult literacy, high school graduation rates, and student achievement (Mindes & Morrison 2014). Forty-two states and the District of Columbia have adopted the Common Core State Standards.

At heart, the CCSS focus on college- and career-readiness through rigorous English language arts and mathematics, emphasizing critical thinking and problem solving for real-world issues. Thus, when the Common Core State Standards were published in 2010, an educational reform agenda for K–12 continued with renewed emphasis on a set of national curriculum standards (NGA & CCSO 2010). That same year, the National Council for the Social Studies (NCSS) started work on *Social Studies for the Next Generation: Purposes, Practices, and Implications of the College, Career, and Civic Life (C3) Framework for Social Studies State Standards* (C3 Framework) (NCSS 2013). The CCSS and the C3 Framework influence how states think about the content and standards for social studies from grades K–12. The C3 Framework proposes standards to help support the development of thinking citizens who participate in a democracy. Close examination of the CCSS and the C3 Framework shows that both documents incorporate many developmentally appropriate practice principles by emphasizing critical thinking and real-world problem solving.

In addition to the Common Core State Standards and the C3 Framework—both of which influence social studies teaching in the early years and beyond—some states are creating social and emotional learning standards. Research shows that children who attend schools with programs teaching social-emotional skills demonstrate improved social behavior and academic achievement, as well as reduced emotional stress and behavior problems (CASEL 2014). The best of these programs are developmentally appropriate, shape school climate, and teach specific skills.

An example of one such program is Recognizing, Understanding, Labeling, Expressing, and Regulating Emotions (RULER), an approach developed by the Yale Center for Emotional Intelligence (Brackett et al. 2011). This program is holistic in that all members of the school community—staff, faculty, children, and families—learn about emotions and the skills to regulate them. RULER affects the overall school climate by involving everyone in thinking about emotions and behaviors that are appropriate for all aspects of school, community, and home life. Practical strategies implemented in the classroom include use of a mood meter by all members of the school community to assess their emotions throughout the day. They develop a vocabulary to describe feelings, as well as skills to moderate strong emotions. The program is developmentally appropriate because it starts where the learner is functioning and scaffolds emotional self-awareness and social-emotional skills application. It puts emotional intelligence research into practice.

Many of RULER's practices are familiar to early childhood teachers. One example is starting the social studies in the early years with a look at the self, the family, and the community. Development of emotional intelligence connects to social studies curriculum through attention to self-awareness in a group setting, and it supports young children's development of citizenship skills and later understandings of the principles of a democratic society.

Teachers begin connecting students to classroom society by supporting the development of social and emotional skills and making connections to social studies curriculum. Over time, students develop greater and more complex understandings of cultural differences, historical trends, and current events. This approach of connecting personal development to social understandings and social studies content serves as a model for teachers who are looking for ways to implement social studies in the crowded school day while addressing students' social and emotional needs. For example, best practice demands that teachers individualize instruction for all learners, scaffold learning for success, employ the latest research on learning, and use age-appropriate materials and strategies (Copple & Bredekamp 2009). This includes appreciating the bond between family and child, recognizing social and cultural contexts, and establishing trust and respect with families (Feeney, Freeman, & Pizzolongo 2012). Educators can "empower children intellectually, socially, emotionally, and politically by using cultural referents to impart skills and attitudes" (Ladson-Billings 1994, 17–18).

Best Practices and Social Studies Projects

The first-graders are considering what it means to be responsible peers in their classroom community. They demonstrate ways to show respect for others by listening when someone is speaking, managing their classroom space, and expressing their opinions. Several children focus on ways to manage conflict. Conversations about these social and emotional skills begin where the children are developmentally and lead to the introduction of a theme on citizenship. The connection to citizenship is linked to recent elections for the local mayor and aldermen and to candidates' announcements for the upcoming presidential election. The class explores elections and reads *Duck for President*, by Doreen Cronin, as well as nonfiction books on elections and citizenship. They develop podcast campaigns, build PowerPoint presentations, hold elections, and demonstrate in other ways their beginning knowledge, skills, and dispositions related to citizenship and democratic principles.

Teachers can prepare children to address the social studies standards by using developmentally appropriate application of the C3 Framework, which addresses history, geography, civics, and economics (NCSS 2013). While state standards differ—particularly for the requirements of local history—the discipline, knowledge, skills, and dispositions can apply to a wide range of the 10 themes from the NCSS (2010). (See the box on this page.) Using the lens of developmentally appropriate practice, which encourages recognizing the social and cultural context of learners and promotes meeting children's learning agendas as individuals, teachers can create engaging content and lessons that are thematically driven using the English language arts and mathematics CCSS benchmarks to plan units on various topics.

10 Themes of Social Studies From the NCSS

1. Culture
2. Time, Continuity, and Change
3. People, Places, and Environment
4. Individual Development and Identity
5. Individuals, Groups, and Institutions
6. Power, Authority, and Governance
7. Production, Distribution, and Consumption
8. Science, Technology, and Society
9. Global Connections
10. Civic Ideals and Practices

(NCSS 2010)

For example, children might study topics such as Chicago, My Kind of Town; National Parks in Our Region; Communication Methods Before Cell Phones; and How Food Gets to Grocery Stores. Or they might search for answers to questions such as: What can we do about abandoned puppies? Why do geese stay in a cold climate when they used to migrate? Where do people work in our community? Where does medicine come from? Why do we vote? Children can investigate each of these questions, which may reflect their own curiosity and specified curriculum content in the primary years, through children's literature, primary documents, oral history, and digital media. As a result, they develop discipline knowledge, skills, and dispositions, and the investigations cross elementary content lines (e.g., math, science, literature, and the social studies).

By investigating these questions, students can apply social studies discipline skills: they can draw maps, explore Google Earth, read history, listen to recorded interviews, graph data, and create charts. Especially rich social studies resources are available through children's literature (see the box on page 84), digital resources adapted for children by National Geographic for Kids (http://kids.nationalgeographic.com), and pictures,

music, maps, and many other primary documents from the Library of Congress (www. loc.gov/education). Access to these resources promotes interesting research questions for children to investigate and builds their discipline knowledge through the implementation of thematic or cross-curricular units, thus developing the dispositions of social studies.

"Teaching" the Social Studies

During the primary years teachers have the opportunity to mentor students, facilitating their social and emotional development and growth. This mentoring includes setting up routines, planning transitions, involving students in developing classroom rules and expectations for behavior, scaffolding interactions among students, and guiding individuals and groups in the use of conflict-resolution strategies. All of these facilitate students' social competence. Also, teachers demonstrate and model respect for all and suggest language to mediate and solve problems, which contributes to children's social and emotional learning and the foundation for civic engagement and self-empowered learning. In addition to building relationships that set the stage for empowered learning, teachers set the stage for the classroom environment—modeling organization and creating stimulating learning centers that change as the content of the student investigations of social studies topics evolve.

Finally, regular collaboration with families fosters students' social development and enhances their social and cultural knowledge. It is important for teachers to include families in classroom activities through conversations by phone, email, or text or in person, and by sharing information on social media and in newsletters. Families and teachers can also

Best Practice in Primary Curriculum Development

Many schools and school districts review and plan with teams of teachers and a curriculum map. The curriculum map identifies all of the standards that must be implemented in a grade level. In developing the map, teachers look for redundancies, gaps, and inconsistencies across the K–3 span, always with an eye toward developmentally appropriate practice. Once the outcomes for grade levels are identified and appropriate assessment guidelines developed, the teams examine ways to promote engaged learning.

One of the best ways to involve learners in critical thinking and meaningful examination of the content of the social studies—history, geography, economics, and civics—is to offer themes of study and projects that promote access to concepts in differentiated ways. The themes often explored in the primary years are community, local history, food distribution, and transportation (and those described in the accompanying article). These overarching themes can be used from year to year with modifications that reflect changes in the community or events in children's lives. For example, if a bridge is closing in the community, as part of the big idea of "moving from place to place," children may have questions, including

> Why is the bridge closing?

> How are bridges built?

> How do they decide where to build the bridge?

> How will this affect traffic?

In accomplishing the goals of this thematic unit and others that are mapped to the K–3 social studies standards, children's books are important resources for helping children explore the topic. The use of children's literature also helps teachers meet the English Language Arts Standards of the Common Core State Standards. Described below are examples of newly available children's literature that support the social studies and that children at various reading levels can access.

Funny Bones: Posada and His Day of the Dead Calaveras
Duncan Tonatiuh. 2015. Abrams.

A funny and sometimes scary story about the Mexican artist José Guadalupe Posada, whose *calaveras*—skeletons performing everyday activities—are now part of Mexico's celebration of Día de los Muertos (Day of the Dead). The story highlights Tonatiuh's art as well as Posada's. The book includes a bibliography, glossary, and index.
Topics: geography, history

How Jelly Roll Morton Invented Jazz
Jonah Winter. Illus. by Keith Mallett. 2015. Roaring Brook Press.

Born Ferdinand Joseph La Menthe in the late 1890s in New Orleans, Jelly Roll Morton was a gifted musician from an early age. A colorful character in the history of American music, Jelly Roll Morton is considered the first jazz composer. The book weaves an enticing look at a dynamic African American cultural contribution to the United States.
Topics: civics, economics, geography, history

My Name Is Truth: The Life of Sojourner Truth
Ann Turner. Illus. by James Ransome. 2015. HarperCollins.

This is the story of how former slave Isabella Baumfree escaped slavery and became the preacher and orator Sojourner Truth, an influential and inspiring member of the abolitionist and women's rights movements. With illustrations that complement the powerful text, this moving book includes historical research, a photo, and suggestions for additional books to read.
Topics: civics, economics, geography, history

Out of the Woods: A True Story of an Unforgettable Event
Rebecca Bond. 2015. Farrar Straus Giroux.

In 1914 in Ontario, Canada, Antonio Giroux's mother ran a hotel on the shores of Gowanda Lake. Antonio's social life revolved around the hotel workers, lumberjacks, and travelers passing through. He spent many hours in the deep woods searching for animals and their tracks. A dry summer resulted in a forest fire, forcing the animals and people into the lake for safety. Remarkably, the animals, hotel workers, and lumberjacks stood side by side peacefully until the fire abated.
Topics: economics, geography, history, economics

Winnie: The True Story of the Bear Who Inspired Winnie-the-Pooh
Sally M. Walker. Illus. by Jonathan D. Voss. 2015. Henry Holt.

Finding Winnie: The True Story of the World's Most Famous Bear
Lindsay Mattick. Illus. by Sophie Blackall. 2015. Hachette.

This is an unusual year in that there are two books about the origins of the real Winnie-the-Pooh. Harry Colburn was a Canadian veterinarian being sent to England to care for horses needed in World War I. At a train stop in Winnipeg, Canada, he noticed a bear cub cowering under a bench. Surmising that the cub needed help, Harry smuggled it onto the train car and eventually all the way to the training camp in England. He named the cub Winnie for Winnipeg. Winnie was given to a London zoo when Harry was deployed to France. It is at the zoo that Christopher Robin and his father, A.A. Milne, made friends with the real Winnie.
Topics: civics, geography, history

To find more children's literature featuring fiction and nonfiction materials to support social studies themes, consult *Horn Book Magazine* (www.hbook.com/horn-book-magazine-2/) and the Notable Social Studies Trade Books for Young People, an annual reading list of exceptional books for use in K–12 social studies from the Children's Book Council and the National Council for Social Studies (www.socialstudies.org/notable).

Thanks to Isabel Baker, president of the Book Vine for Children, for this selection and description of books. Isabel has worked as a children's librarian and currently presents on early literacy and book selection.

regularly exchange information about students' individual characteristics, and families can serve as resources for cultural and historical content for the thematic investigations and units of the social studies.

Conclusion

Teachers can approach the social studies by starting with students' interests and questions, thus promoting critical thinking, increasing knowledge in social studies domains, and fostering development of social competence. Developmentally appropriate practice in social studies investigations offers a model for implementation of curriculum development and social and emotional learning for all children.

References

Brackett, M.A., J.P. Kremenitzer, M. Maurer, S.E. Rivers, N.A. Elbertson, & M.D. Carpenter, eds. 2011. *Creating Emotionally Literate Classrooms: An Introduction to the RULER Approach to Social and Emotional Learning.* Port Chester, NY: National Professional Resources.

CASEL (Collaborative for Academic, Social, and Emotional Learning). 2014. "Social and Emotional Learning in Policy." www.casel.org/policy.

Copple, C., & S. Bredekamp, eds. 2009. *Developmentally Appropriate Practice in Early Childhood Programs Serving Children From Birth Through Age 8.* 3rd ed. Washington, DC: NAEYC.

Feeney, S., N.K. Freeman, & P.J. Pizzolongo. 2012. *Ethics and the Early Childhood Educator: Using the NAEYC Code.* 2nd ed. Washington, DC: NAEYC.

Ladson-Billings, G. 1994. *The Dreamkeepers: Successful Teachers of African American Children.* San Francisco: Jossey-Bass.

Mindes, G., & G. Morrison. 2014. "Common Core State Standards (CCSS) and Excellence in Early Childhood Education for All Children." Paper presented at the NAEYC Annual Conference & Expo, in Washington, DC, November.

NCSS (National Council for the Social Studies). 2010. *National Curriculum Standards for Social Studies: A Framework for Teaching, Learning, and Assessment.* Silver Spring, MD: NCSS.

NCSS. 2013. *Social Studies for the Next Generation: Purposes, Practices, and Implications of the College, Career, and Civic Life (C3) Framework for Social Studies State Standards.* Silver Spring, MD: NCSS.

NGA (National Governors Association Center for Best Practices) & CCSSO (Council of Chief State School Officers). 2010. *Common Core State Standards.* Washington, DC: NGA & CCSSO. www.corestandards.org.

About the Author

Gayle Mindes, EdD, is professor of education at DePaul University in Chicago, where she teaches in the preservice early childhood and elementary education programs. A lifelong urban educator, Gayle writes and speaks on assessment, social studies, and kindergarten. The second edition of her book *Social Studies for Young Children: Preschool and Primary Curriculum Anchor* was published recently. Gayle is a member of NAEYC's consulting editors panel.

Guiding Children's Friendship Development

Kathleen Cranley Gallagher

In Jessie and Alex's first grade classroom, the children choose from several activities. A few play a board game they have created, others work on a large jigsaw puzzle, and several contribute to a class thank-you note in the writing center. Several children gather around the terrarium to see if the caterpillar has made progress toward becoming a butterfly. For some children, discussions become emotional, with emphatic assertions of rightness, fairness, and turn taking. A few children reference classroom rules, displayed on a wall, and most disagreements result in children negotiating harmonious outcomes. The teachers take turns supporting children's interactions and helping them work out rightness and fairness issues. Jessie and Alex do not worry when children argue—they see these occasions as learning opportunities.

As part of Morning Meeting, the teachers present a short lesson on strategies for being a good friend, providing time for role play and practice. Each day they include lessons for supporting children's interpersonal skills, and they design learning opportunities to engage all learners, offering strategies to engage peers who are not usually included in social activities.

The ability to make and retain friends impacts children's development in important ways and is associated with positive social-emotional health through childhood and into adulthood. Children without friends, who are rejected or neglected by peers, often have poor self-regulation and communication skills and more challenging behaviors (Ladd, Herald, & Andrews 2006). Kindergarten and primary classrooms and after-school programs provide ideal contexts for learning to develop friendships; however, teachers receive little initial training or professional development related to this essential part of the curriculum (Gallagher et al. 2007; Gallagher & Sylvester 2009). In this article readers will learn some effective strategies to help children of all abilities, ages 6–9 years, develop friendships.

Social-Emotional Development in the Primary Years

Young children experience their world as an environment of relationships that affect virtually all aspects of their development. Focusing on children's relationships, and friendships in particular, builds a foundation of social competence and positive behavior. However, children's social skills do not just emerge naturally. As with academic learning, social-emotional learning develops in the context of a positive environment in which adults nurture supportive relationships with children, scaffold children's skills, and use direct instruction to teach specific social skills and foster positive relationships.

Understanding of Self, of Emotions, and of Emotional Regulation

In the primary grades, children develop increased self-understanding and express preferences, dislikes, and characteristics more clearly and effectively than younger children. They engage in social comparison that manifests itself as ideas about equality and fairness: "Sarah got an extra turn; I should too." Children also begin to use social comparison to gauge their own skills: "Bruno is a fast runner; I'm not so fast."

Most children this age understand that they can have mixed emotions about an event, like feeling both excited and a little scared at the beginning of a new school year. With a more complex understanding of feelings, they can regulate their emotions more effectively (Berk 2012). This is reflected in primary school children having fewer emotional outbursts than preschoolers. Some children are temperamentally more prone to anxiety and fearfulness, and experience emotions more intensely than other children. They may react angrily when frustrated and thus damage their relationships with peers and teachers.

Understanding Others

Most children in the primary grades demonstrate understanding of others' perspectives. They begin to realize that people receive and interpret information differently and therefore may come to different conclusions. Children who see others' perspectives may show more sensitivity toward others' feelings; as a result, they are more skilled in social interactions and tend to have more positive relationships with peers (Berk 2012).

Important Teacher Understandings

These are some assumptions to guide you when integrating friendship development in primary grade curricula:

> All children deserve the right to learn and interact with peers.

> All children need friends.

> Developing friendships comes more easily for some children than for others.

> Those who work with young children have a responsibility to help them develop friendships.

> You can support children's friendship development by adapting the setting and activities so that all children can participate fully.

Six- to 9-year-olds understand social expectations, including rules and cultural conventions (Copple & Bredekamp 2009). They develop a sense of social justice and recognize rules as important. They understand that intending to violate a rule, and then doing so, is worse than violating a rule accidentally. At this age, children begin to predict how their actions will make other people, including peers, feel.

Social-emotional understanding is widely variable; children's temperaments and cognitive abilities, and their parents' childrearing skills, are all related to how children understand themselves and others, as are family and cultural values and expectations. From this knowledge about the social-emotional understanding of 6- to 9-year-olds, teachers can think about how to support and extend children's social relationships, specifically their friendships.

Friendship is a particularly complex type of social relationship because it requires reciprocal positive regard, trust, and shared interests (Gallagher et al. 2007; Gallagher & Sylvester 2009). In past decades, society held that socialization in the early years was the responsibility of the family, and the school's responsibility was to focus on children's academic growth and learning. Yet children's social, academic, and physical aspects of learning and development are all linked (Denham & Brown 2010). Many skills are needed for children to successfully build and nurture friendships, and several variables affect this process.

For some teachers, it can be overwhelming to think about supporting children's social-emotional learning. They wonder how to assess where each child is in social-emotional learning, how to provide a supportive environment so friendships can develop, how to help children learn what to do so friendships can develop, and how to support children who struggle to develop friendships (Gallagher et al. 2007).

A Pyramid Model for Supporting Friendship Development

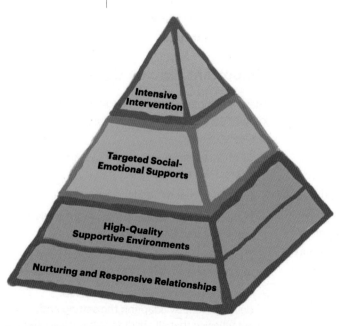

One tool to help teachers think about, plan for, and implement social-emotional learning and friendship development is a pyramid model (Hemmeter, Fox, & Snyder 2013). When using this pyramid to guide social-emotional learning, the teacher establishes high-quality relationships with children and creates an environment to support children's social learning and relationships. She observes to understand where the children are in their development. The information she gains from observation informs her teaching and lets her individualize as necessary. The pyramid's four tiers include universal practices (first two levels from the bottom up) that teachers use with all children. The third tier includes practices that teach strategies to support relationships and prevent challenges. And the final tier includes more intensive interventions for children who are struggling with relationships and behavior.

Pyramid illustration reprinted with permission from the Center on the Social and Emotional Foundations for Early Learning (CSEFEL), Vanderbilt University, Nashville, Tennessee.

Establishing Relationships

Developmentally appropriate environmental and relational supports in the classroom form the base of the model. For friendship development, this means setting up environments to support warm relationships: modeling nurturing behaviors, setting expectations, establishing rules for interactions with others, and making emotional literacy a central part of the curriculum. Essentially, it is important to establish a warm, safe, and caring classroom climate and high expectations for respectful and kind interactions.

To build relationships with children, primary teachers engage in conversations with children, use encouraging language, and provide assistance so children with special needs can communicate. For example, a teacher might use circle time to have conversations about friendship and use a talking stick to ensure that every child has a chance to speak. The teacher may build time into her weekly schedule to have a short conversation with each child. She may build a brief, informal discussion into small group activities, allowing children to connect with her and with each other.

> Jessie and Alex build individualized good-byes into the end of the day. Regardless of what the day has brought, as the children line up to leave, their teachers give each child a warm hug or a thumbs-up to remind the children that they are cherished and that their return the next day will be a fresh start.

The foundation level of the pyramid is the one in which teachers also develop relationships with families. Opportunities for family engagement, communication, and support should be integrated into the classroom. Many elementary schools offer a few opportunities each year for family engagement and participation. Teachers have often shared with me that it is always the same families that participate. A key to expanding family participation is to vary and increase the type and level of communication. This can be difficult to manage for a class of more than 20 children! A personal short note or email every few weeks highlighting some achievement or special moment is powerful ("Alisha is growing in so many ways this year! She is enjoying heading our class garden and writing stories about animals with Miguel."). One parent said that when his child's teacher started doing this, he began to believe that the teacher knew the child well, and he felt more comfortable when he visited the classroom.

High-Quality Environmental Supports

The second level of the pyramid, supporting high-quality environments, should also be part of the general classroom climate and curriculum. When teachers plan for their environment, they can ensure that there are sufficient materials for children to use and set up classroom furniture and learning centers to support opportunities for children to collaborate.

> Jessie and Alex have arranged the writing center so that children face each other. They pair children for writing time and includes story starters. These are designed to prompt children to discuss and learn about each other—for example, "Write about your partner's favorite pet" and "Tell about your favorite food and your partner's favorite food. Are they the same or different?"

Teachers include children in developing guidelines for the classroom community. Teachers may institute practices designed to have children collaborate, such as asking a friend for help before asking a teacher.

> Jessie and Alex have introduced the practice "Ask three and then ask me." When children ask for help, the teachers encourage them to first find a classmate who might help. However, the children know that if they ask three classmates and still need assistance, the teachers will help. Jessie and Alex monitor this carefully to be sure children don't get too frustrated, but they have noticed children's increased confidence in their ability to help others, solve problems, and build relationships around helping each other.

Another important part of high-quality environmental support is carefully designing and structuring transitions so children don't have to wait too long with nothing to do. Typically during unstructured times, some children wander, others patiently wait, and a few find interesting ways to create adventure—often at the expense of order and harmony.

> Jessie and Alex use transitions to support friendships and expand learning. They assign children a weekly buddy, and the children partner with their buddy during classroom transitions. Jessie and Alex have named the transitions (lunchtime transition, centers transition) and explained their

Reflection Questions

The information and strategies in this article will help you adapt your curriculum, environment, and practices to support each student's social and emotional growth, particularly their capacity for developing friendships. To review and expand on the ideas presented, consider these questions.

1. Why is it important to support the development of friendships for students in the primary grades?

2. What are some supports you might use in your classroom at each tiered level? What would you need to implement them?

3. What social skills might you provide direct instruction on? How could you provide this instruction?

4. What are some strategies you might use to intentionally support the friendship development of children with disabilities, while meeting the needs of all children?

expectations for each. They use musical cues to let children know when it's time to transition to a different center; lights for transitions requiring quiet gatherings; and poems and recitations (counting by 5s) to move from one part of the building to another. For times requiring silent or quiet moving through the halls, the teachers engage the children by performing finger actions to favorite poems. With their line partner, children do the finger actions while moving in the hall.

Targeted Social-Emotional Supports

At the third level of the pyramid, teachers offer targeted social-emotional supports. This includes direct instruction to all children in social-emotional skills used to form friendships, and individual or small group instruction to support children who need a bit more assistance and practice. Teachers may help children learn how to identify and express emotions and how to use strategies to manage anger and excitement, collaborate with peers, and build friendship skills. Because primary-age children have a more sophisticated understanding of reality and fantasy and are developing an understanding of multiple perspectives, role playing can be a particularly powerful strategy.

Alex has noticed that the children are often unable to effectively communicate with words in situations involving strong emotions. To accommodate the different levels of children's development in the class, Alex adapted Tucker Turtle (see csefel.vanderbilt.edu/resources/strategies.html) to work with the children on managing strong emotions. Teaching the children to "Take 5," Alex incorporates Tucker Turtle's essential skills: (1) stop, (2) take a still stance, and (3, 4, and 5) take three breaths. As a group, they practice this strategy, role-play scenarios with partners, and coach each other in its use.

When situations call for cooler heads, Alex and Jessie remind the children to take 5, and then other children take over. Whether the children are in the classroom, in the lunchroom, or on the playground, they can be heard reminding each other to take 5 when interactions get heated. Alex and Jessie are pleased when the strategy works with the group, but they are elated by the transformation that emerges for one child with autism. For Ben, "Take 5" is magic. He uses the strategy daily, with reminders from teachers, classmates, and himself. Using "Take 5," Ben puts his strong reactions in check and begins problem solving—with help at first, and eventually independently. Alex and Jessie note that this is Ben's first step in forming friendships with classmates—something that up until this point has eluded him.

Supporting Friendships Among Dual Language Learners

Wondering how to encourage children who speak different languages to build friendships? Try these suggestions.

› Teach all of the children skills that help them communicate with someone who speaks another language, such as speaking slowly but not in an exaggerated way, repeating, using lots of gestures, and demonstrating what they are trying to communicate.

› Plan cooperative activities and games that encourage working together and having fun, such as painting a large mural together or planting a garden. Assign children buddies so they can get to know each other and help each other. These activities encourage children to learn the value of each other's friendship across language barriers.

› If you have a "lunch with the teacher" tradition, in each group include children whose home languages are different. Facilitate conversations and focus on social interactions. Model your willingness to try to learn a child's language by asking him or her to teach you a few words.

› Share books and stories about characters who are different but who learn to appreciate each others' differences and enjoy working and playing together. Where possible, provide books in the languages of the children in your class.

› Work with parents in a variety of ways. Let every family know that your goal is to encourage all the children in the class to get along.

There are many level 3 strategies teachers can use to help children learn the skills they need in order to develop and sustain friendships. *Meet Thotso, Your Thought Maker,* by Rachel Robb Avery, is a book designed to help children process and express strong emotions and develop affirming thoughts. In it, Thotso the Brain teaches children about positive thinking skills, and how children can turn BooBoo Thots (that make you feel bad) into Smiling Thots (that make you feel good) by using Bandage Thots (caring phrases that you can say to yourself).

Because children at these ages play and enjoy games with rules, board games—purchased or teacher designed—are an effective way to support friendships. Games help children learn strategies for handling winning and losing, taking turns, waiting, and encouraging others. In the game Ring Bling, children develop their listening skills as they solve social challenges and earn rings to put on cardboard hands—or on their own. Children may at first need adults to provide more support during social board games, but eventually they will require little adult monitoring.

Jessie and Alex often use games to reinforce academic goals. The children—especially Ben—love board and card games of all kinds; however, playing games sometimes results in disagreements or thrown pieces. Jessie and Alex see an opportunity to enhance friendship relationships by teaching Ben and the other children language associated with playing games. They have the children practice and role-play saying encouraging phrases like "Good move," "Try again," and "Oh well, maybe next time" as they show children that winning and losing are both okay outcomes. As with many of the strategies they implement, this one works well for all the children, decreasing conflicts in their relationships. However, it especially supports Ben in his relationships. With these new language skills, Ben's competitive edge softens, and the other children are more eager to play games with him.

Teachers help children learn how to identify and reach out to peers who may need friendship support. One strategy involves teaching children to "Stop, look around, and see who is not having fun" (Wong & Gallagher 2012). Teachers present the steps in small or large groups, and children practice them using role play. This is a particularly powerful way to help children notice others who are isolated and to provide opportunities for children to invite them to join an activity.

Using another strategy, Buddy Play (Odom et al. 2006), children learn to initiate interactions with another child. This is particularly effective for children with special needs. During games or other activities or at recess, children use the three steps Stay, Play, and Talk:

> Stay—be close to your buddy and go where he wants to play

> Play—share, take turns, bring a game or activity over and ask a buddy to play with you

> Talk—find things to say about the activity or about the buddy

One thing Jessie and Alex have learned with their class is never to assume they have it all figured out. As they teach new friendship skills and help children integrate them into their relationships, new challenges arise. They know that this is part of social-emotional learning, and that they will always need to expand their toolkit of practices. When they find themselves struggling to support children, they sometimes turn to a colleague who specializes in positive behavior support.

Intensive Interventions

Incorporating practices from the first three pyramid levels supports development of friendships and prevents and addresses most relationship problems in classrooms. However, some children have more serious difficulties with relationships. They may have a disability that interferes with their communication or problem-solving skills. They may be processing a traumatic experience. These children need specially designed opportunities to learn and practice specific social skills.

Though some teachers develop individualized, positive-behavior support plans on their own or with a teaching partner, many work with a specialist and the child's family to individualize more intensive interventions. This level involves data collection, strategies targeted for individual children, opportunities to practice, and progress monitoring. It often helps to have a consultant's viewpoint on challenging situations. Teachers can implement many of the same practices used at other levels of the pyramid in this level, but they need to be implemented more intensively (more frequently, one-to-one) and carefully monitored to assess children's progress.

Conclusion

In developing friendships, children learn important cognitive skills such as perspective taking, problem solving, and pattern recognition (such as in turn taking). By practicing conflict resolution and negotiation in safe relationships, children learn to feel sympathy for and empathy with others and build their friendship skills. When children learn about emotions, practice identifying them, and deepen their understanding of them, children learn to focus and redirect negative emotions. Of course, teachers can more effectively support children's friendship development if complementary policies and practices are in place at the school and community levels. Furthermore, it is important for teachers to engage families in developing expectations and practices related to their children's social relationships. When families, teachers, and schools work together to provide a foundation for friendship development, children benefit in ways that support lifelong health and success.

Selected Resources for Supporting Children's Friendships

Teaching Children About Friendship/Relationships

Paley, V.G. 1993. *You Can't Say You Can't Play.* Boston: Harvard University Press.

Research

Dunlap, G., & D. Powell. 2009. *Promoting Social Behavior of Young Children in Group Settings: A Summary of Research.* Tampa: University of South Florida, Technical Assistance Center on Social Emotional Intervention for Young Children. www.challengingbehavior.org/do/ resources/documents/roadmap_3.pdf.

Collaborative for Academic, Social, and Emotional Learning (CASEL). 2012. *Effective Social and Emotional Learning Programs: Preschool and Elementary School Edition.* Chicago: CASEL.

http://static1.squarespace.com/static/513f79f9e4b05ce7b70e9673/t/526a220de4b00a92c90436ba/1382687245993/ 2013-casel-guide.pdf.

Web-Based Teaching Strategies/Lesson Plans

Center on the Social and Emotional Foundations for Early Learning. "Resources: Practical Strategies for Teachers/Caregivers." http://csefel.vanderbilt.edu/resources/strategies.html#list

Responsive Classroom. www.responsiveclassroom.org/aboutresponsive-classroom

BrainPOP, Jr. "Lesson Ideas: Friends." www.brainpop.com/educators/community/bp-jr-topic/friends

Bucket Fillers. www.bucketfillers101.com/free-resources.php

Children's Books

Feelings, by Aliki

Those Shoes, by Maribeth Boelts

The Name Jar, by Yangsook Choi

Do Unto Otters: A Book About Manners, by Laurie Keller

Have You Filled a Bucket Today? A Guide to Daily Happiness for Kids, by Carol McCloud

How Full Is Your Bucket? For Kids, by Tom Rath and Mary Reckmeyer

Should I Share My Ice Cream?, by Mo Willems

Each Kindness, by Jacqueline Woodson

References

Berk, L.E. 2012. *Infants and Children: Prenatal Through Middle Childhood.* 7th ed. New York: Pearson.

Copple, C., & S. Bredekamp, eds. 2009. *Developmentally Appropriate Practice in Early Childhood Programs Serving Children From Birth Through Age 8.* 3rd ed. Washington, DC: NAEYC.

Denham, S.A., & C. Brown. 2010. "'Plays Nice With Others': Social-Emotional Learning and Academic Success." *Early Education and Development* 21 (5): 652–80.

Gallagher, K., K. Dadisman, T.W. Farmer, L. Huss, & B.C. Hutchins. 2007. "Social Dynamics of Early Childhood Classrooms: Considerations and Implications for Teachers." Chap. 3 in *Contemporary Perspectives on Social Learning in Early Childhood Education,* eds. O.N. Saracho & B. Spodek. Greenwich, CT: Information Age.

Gallagher, K.C., & P.R. Sylvester. 2009. "Supporting Peer Relationships in Early Education." Chap. 11 in *Handbook of Child Development and Early Education: Research to Practice,* eds. O. Barbarin & B.H. Wasik. New York: Guilford.

Hemmeter, M.L., L. Fox, & P. Snyder. 2013. "A Tiered Model for Promoting Social-Emotional Competence and Addressing Challenging Behavior." Chap. 6 in *Handbook of Response to Intervention in Early Childhood,* eds. V. Buysse & E.S. Peisner-Feinberg. Baltimore: Paul H. Brookes Publishing Co.

Ladd, G.W., S.L. Herald, & R.K. Andrews. 2006. "Young Children's Peer Relations and Social Competence." Chap. 2 in *Handbook of Research on the Education of Young Children,* 2nd ed., eds. B. Spodek & O.N. Saracho. Mahwah, NJ: Erlbaum.

Odom, S.L., C. Zercher, S. Li, J.M. Marquart, S. Sandall, & W.H. Brown. 2006. "Social Acceptance and Rejection of Preschool Children With Disabilities: A Mixed-Method Analysis." *Journal of Educational Psychology* 98 (4): 807–23.

Wong, C., & K. Gallagher. 2012. "Preschool Inclusion Project." Manual. Chapel Hill: University of North Carolina at Chapel Hill.

About the Author

Kathleen Cranley Gallagher, PhD, is an educational psychologist and scientist at the Frank Porter Graham (FPG) Child Development Institute at the University of North Carolina at Chapel Hill. Her research and professional development pursuits focus on supporting children's early relationships in the contexts of family and early childhood program settings.

"We're Many Members, but One Body": Fostering a Healthy Self-Identity and Agency in African American Boys

Brian L. Wright, Shelly L. Counsell, and Shelby L. Tate

Kevin's classroom dilemma

A White second grade teacher at a predominantly White university campus laboratory school contacts an African American mother to request a meeting to discuss her son Kevin's behavior. When Kevin's parents arrive for the afternoon meeting, they can see that their son is visibly upset. To calm him down, Kevin's father walks him to the boys' restroom while his mother remains in the classroom with the teacher to discuss what happened.

The teacher tells Kevin's mother that her son got out of his seat without permission. When he was told to sit back down, he insisted he needed to sharpen his pencil. "When I told Kevin to use another pencil, he slammed his pencil on his desktop in defiance."

When Kevin and his father return from the restroom, they join the conversation. Kevin's mother turns to him and states, "Your teacher told me that you have been disrespectful." Kevin says, "No, Mama, you don't understand." She responds, "I'm not going to tolerate your being disrespectful." He says, "I raised my hand holding my pencil because I needed to sharpen it. She told me to put my hand down. I then raised my hand again and propped my knee on my chair and said, 'I need to sharpen my pencil.' She told me to sit in my chair and put my hand down. I slammed my hand down [in frustration] holding the pencil and it rolled off my desk." Kevin's mother repeats, "It doesn't matter. I'm not going to tolerate your being disrespectful."

Again Kevin says, "No, Mama, you don't understand" and starts crying. His mother pauses, looks at her son with great concern, and says, "What is going on?" Kevin continues, "Mama, she treats Black kids and Mexican kids differently." With a son growing up Black and male in the United States, Kevin's mother and father have engaged in ongoing conversations about race and discrimination, always reassuring their son that he has the same rights as other children who do not look like him. His mother reminds him, as she has done many times before, "What have I taught you? We all bleed the same blood." Her son says, "Yes, Mama. We all bleed the same blood," as he continues to cry. His mother comforts him by saying, "We're many members, but one body."

Kevin's mother turns to the teacher and asks, "Is this true?" The teacher says, "Oh, Kevin, I am so sorry you feel that way. I've heard this from other students, and I hate that you all feel that way."

While this incident could happen to a child from a different cultural group, the frequency with which African American boys experience such treatment in schools (not to mention outside of school) far exceeds that of children from other racial and ethnic groups (see Barbarin & Crawford 2006; Davis 2005; Wright 2011). The unique challenges and complex ways in which structural racism, including both implicit bias and explicit forms of racism, shapes the experiences and well-being of African American males must be considered and understood.

A Closer Look at Black Boys

The opening vignette exemplifies the running narrative of the educational experiences of many Black boys in US classrooms, past and present. Research shows that, all too often, boys are viewed as problems in school (Barbarin & Crawford 2006). In another study spanning the primary school years, Barbarin (2013) found that boys of color (specifically African American boys) are subject to

disproportionately high rates of disciplinary action, such as suspensions and expulsions. These actions, combined with the ways that Black boys are socially and culturally misunderstood, result in misguided school practices that often disadvantage African American boys in punitive ways (Barbarin 2010; Wright 2011).

Beginning in preschool, some teachers tend to stigmatize African American boys, giving them negative labels, such as "bad boy" or "troublemaker," that are often passed along from teacher to teacher throughout a child's schooling. Labels such as these lead to isolation and exclusion from classroom activities. Disturbingly, they are also picked up by other children and perceived as truth (Barbarin & Crawford 2006). Over time, the impact of these labels affects societal expectations of African American boys and, at times, expectations they have for themselves, both social and academic (Harper & Associates 2014). In contrast to these trends, positive racial identities among African American boys contribute strongly to high academic achievement (Wright 2011). Unfortunately, too many boys do not find the needed encouragement to develop healthy identities, self-esteem, and social competence in early childhood settings.

Some African American boys' styles of communication and interaction in learning environments are at odds with mainstream discourse and interaction. For example, children may bring different dialects and languages (e.g., African American English, Spanish, American slang) to the classroom that are not aligned with Standard English. Such linguistic practices intersect race and gender in ways that tend to limit the educational experiences and opportunities of African American boys (Wright 2011). As noted by Barbarin and Crawford (2006), "When African American children in general, and boys in particular, are stigmatized, it seems imperative to consider the role of race" (82). Healthy relationships between teachers and students support the development of positive identities, self-esteem, and social competence in and outside classrooms (Hamre & Pianta 2001).

Self-Identity, Agency, and Community

Self-identity answers the question "Who am I?" Who we are distinguishes us from everyone else in the world. Children learn about themselves and construct their own self-identity in the context of their families and communities. Tennessee's academic standards for second grade social studies suggest the role of the teacher is to help students understand their self-identity as American citizens (Tennessee Department of Education 2013). Students explore the ways "we are all part of the same community, sharing principles, goals, and traditions despite varied ancestry" (p. 1) while also identifying the rights and actions of citizens of the United States. For example, second-graders in Memphis could research the community decision to dedicate art murals at the Willow Park and Pine Hill Community Center. The mural "This Is My Song," by Kyle Taylor and Chad M. Irwin, represents the generations—youth, adulthood, and the elderly—in their journey to live life well and in pursuit of education (Urban Art 2014). Similarly, a second grade teacher could designate a classroom bulletin board for student-selected topics and themes. Every month, children could vote on a new topic, theme, or purpose. Students might vote to use the bulletin board to showcase an "I Have a Dream" theme with real-life neighborhood parks in the surrounding community, proposing project ideas for how to make them better. Students could then vote on which community project they want to complete as a class.

Applying these academic standards to the early childhood classroom supports the development of a democratic learning community in which each child's self-identity is recognized, valued, and reflected. Moreover, in such a classroom community, children are granted choices and are encouraged to responsibly make decisions that consider the individual and collective good of the group. These kinds of activities provide students with firsthand experiences in a deliberative, decision-making process (agency). According to Howard, Rose, and Barbarin (2013), when children experience healthy environments and positive relationships, they see themselves as important members of a community that values, cares about, and respects them, thus creating a sense of belonging.

Agency answers the questions "What actions can I take?" and "Will my actions make a difference?" Children's ability to act upon their cultural worlds of home and school is one example of agency. Agency is a child's ability to construct and co-construct his environment by negotiating different courses of action. For example, when children choose among different learning center activities or negotiate parts in a skit, they exercise agency by problem solving to satisfy the needs of individuals and of the group as a whole.

Guided by questions of self-identity and agency, how can teachers engage young children, especially Black boys, in the development of a positive self-identity? To begin to answer this question, we turn to the work of Derman-Sparks and Edwards (2010), who state that in their vision of anti-bias education, "all children and families have a sense of belonging and experience affirmation of their identities and cultural ways of being" (2). To help African American boys experience affirmation of self-identity, we recommend an authentic social studies teaching approach from a "history and me" perspective. This curriculum approach should be one that reflects, represents, and celebrates a vision for social change in America forged historically by all Americans, with a particular emphasis on African Americans.

The Tennessee social studies academic standards for second grade include a focus on government, civics, and history (Tennessee Department of Education 2013). Children study who they are as Americans, including the rights and privileges guaranteed to all US citizens. Second-graders are expected to develop an appreciation and respect for different cultures, and to explain the ways in which we are all part of the same community. Children's understanding of community includes both the neighborhood in which they live and the learning community they experience at school.

In alignment with the Tennessee social studies standards, we provide strategies to promote self-identity, agency, and a sense of classroom community. We do so with the understanding that to interpret and/or reduce the experiences of Kevin and many children like him into a set of best practices may undermine the complexity of the issues. We begin with ways to promote self-identity and agency with children in general and with African American boys in particular, followed by approaches to creating a democratic classroom using "Kevin's Classroom Dilemma" as an example.

History and Me

Applying the "history and me" perspective, teachers provide curricular materials that expose Black boys to a rich and diverse African American history that, for example, focuses on identities of Black boys and men. Such exposure is critical to the boys' development of a healthy sense of self and their ability (and that of other children) to challenge stereotypes such as troublemaker and bad boy, which have become a stable part of the self-identity of African American boys. Reading and discussing picture books that focus on African American males—for example, the biography *Richard Wright and the Library Card* (1997), by William Miller, and the historical fiction *Sit-In: How Four Friends Stood Up by Sitting*

Down (2010), by Andrea Davis Pinkney—fosters the development of positive self-identity and agency.

Mirror Books Versus Window Books

Teachers can contribute to African American boys' discovery of who they are, both historically and culturally, by designing a celebration of self-identity through African American children's literature that ensures that Black boys see themselves in books that introduce them to "mentors on paper" (Thompson 1996). African American boys, perhaps more than any other group of children, need access to what Rudine Sims Bishop (1990) calls *mirror books*. Currently, children of color have far too many *window books*, looking into an all-White world, and far too few mirror books reflecting who they are. Books such as *Freedom Summer* (2005), by Deborah Wiles, and *Delivering Justice: W.W. Law and the Fight for Civil Rights* (2008), by Jim Haskins, provide examples of young African American men whose actions challenged racial discrimination in the South by helping members of their community register to vote and protest peacefully in order to declare that all American citizens are equal.

Belonging and Affirmation

While story time and independent reading are essential parts of daily classroom routines, these alone do not accomplish a sense of belonging and affirmation for African American boys. In other words, "it is critical for children of color to see themselves, their culture, and their perspectives in the books they read" (McNair 2014, 69). For this reason, we recommend active, interactive, and gregarious ways to talk about history and to share mirror books with all children, and Black boys in particular.

Teaching social studies using children's books can include pantomime, choral readings, readers theater, mask making, puppetry, storytelling, and improvisation (Gangi 2004; Rasinski 2010). In addition to being kinesthetic and visual, these arts-based approaches encourage the development of children's self-identity and agency. For example, the children's book *Junebug* (1995), by Alice Mead, is about a young boy who lives in a housing project. At the age of 10, every boy in this housing project is forced to join a gang for "survival." Junebug does not want to join a gang; instead, he wants to move away with his mother and sister to have a better life. Junebug refuses to give up on his dream for a better life. As a motivation, he celebrates his tenth birthday with a collection of glass bottles filled with notes about his dreams and wishes. Teachers can highlight Junebug's determination to hold on to his dreams and explain how his bottle collection represents agency—a child's ability to construct and co-construct his environment through the practice of negotiating different courses of action.

Developing an Empowerment Club for Boys

African American boys can and do benefit from a variety of African American male mentors who offer exposure to a broad range of possibilities. For example, meeting African American men involved in caring professions, such as nursing or teaching, can help boys expand their ideas of what is possible for them. Ongoing exposure to positive male mentors could also result in the design and creation of a boys' empowerment club. Ideally, such a club would be developed collaboratively by teachers and students. The club can serve a variety of purposes. It can take place in different parts of the school (inside and outside) and at different times, even after school. For example, devote a small segment of recess to structured learning games or quick science experiments. The club would be open to all boys, and certainly could be replicated with girls.

Boys might set up ramps of different heights and use toy cars of various sizes. Teachers could ask them to predict how far certain cars will travel on each ramp, and then boys would test their predictions (DeVries & Sales 2011). Teachers also can encourage boys to create other outdoor learning games and science experiments with instructions for other children to follow. Teachers can engage boys in writing and directing a play. This can be a confidence builder and connect to their study of history and exposure to mirror books that authentically reflect and represent African American males. The club can serve as a safe place and space for boys to discuss and share their feelings about school, family, and their community and their hopes and dreams. Finally, a club can provide opportunities for boys to meet and spend time with Black males who are in middle school and high school to learn what to expect when they are in these grades, as well as activities and interests they might like to pursue in and outside of school. The club can also serve as an opportunity to educate boys about college and career opportunities. Clubs can plan a Dress for Success Day, a Father–Son–Mentor Day, or a Boys Reading Day. Implementing these suggestions can contribute to African American boys' sense of self and agency as valued members of their classroom community (Kafele 2009).

Sense of Community and the World

A South African proverb states, "I am, because we are. And because we are, I am." In the tradition of many African societies, there is an emphasis on the collective more than on the individual. Thus, in a democratic classroom community, "Who am I?" and "What is my purpose?" become "Who are we?" and "What is our purpose?" in order to reflect community and affirm the claim made by Kevin's mother that "we're many members, but one body."

When teachers actively listen to, openly acknowledge, and value children's prior knowledge, learning interests, agendas, and ideas, teachers become "fellow travelers" who co-construct meanings with children through a shared learning journey of growth and empowerment. As fellow travelers in the creation of a democratic learning community, teachers and children work together to define how they want to think, speak, act, learn, and grow together.

Democratic classrooms, as described by Kohn (2006), view all students as community members with the opportunity to (a) have a voice in what happens; (b) help shape the course of study; (c) help decide when, where, why, how, and with whom learning takes place; and (d) help decide how progress will be assessed. The learning environment is then designed so young children can explore what interests them, and direct their own activity and decision making (empowerment and agency) by selecting materials and participating in activities in a variety of social arrangements (independent, pairs, small group, and large group).

As an evidence-based teaching strategy, the classroom meeting is a specific learning activity that embodies and promotes self-identity, agency, and democratic learning communities. Teachers use class meetings to give children opportunities to identify issues, reflect on their choices, consider the outcomes that resulted, and make better decisions that value and respect everyone (DSC 1996; Vance 2015). These meetings demonstrate to children that their individual learning, opinions, feelings, concerns, beliefs, and ideas matter (are legitimated) to everyone— especially the teacher. According to the Developmental Studies Center's (DSC 1996) research, class meetings with young children are generally used

Reflective Practitioners

As classroom leaders, teachers can—intentionally and unintentionally—send devastating messages that negatively impact children's self-identity (how the children see and value themselves and each other in the learning community). It is important for teachers to continually contemplate whether they afford all children equal agency for having their voices, feelings, and perspectives respected and valued by the teacher and peers. Reflective practitioners examine (and reexamine), on an ongoing basis, personal and professional values and attitudes that underlie teaching practices. They make a full commitment to promoting and supporting democratic learning communities that grant and guarantee full membership to all children through equal participation, which serves to eliminate classroom stratification based largely on children's race or gender.

Democratic leaders

In light of what Kevin and his classmates could discuss during a class meeting, reflective practitioners would rethink and rework all practices that have resulted in unfair treatment of children based on race. They would need to adopt a positive problem-solving stance in order to come to terms with their own racial and ethnic understanding of others. This requires an honest self-appraisal through examination of personal and professional values that underlie this kind of practice, and a resolve to change their practices in ways that will increase community participation, active decision making, and access to learning opportunities and classroom resources. It is vital for teachers to critically examine their treatment (conscious or unconscious) of children who look like them versus those who do not.

A reflective response

Kevin's teacher could have responded to him in this way: "Oh, Kevin, when I didn't let you [a non-White child] sharpen your pencil, even though I let other children sharpen theirs, it was wrong and unfair. My decision prevented you from having equal access to our class supplies and resources. I should have let you voice your frustration [self-agency] so that you could have problem-solved the situation as a valued community member [deliberative process]. I will work harder to recognize students' pleas to be heard, understood, valued, and appreciated."

Democratic learning environments are considered an essential component of early childhood practice. However, we believe that power dynamics such as race, class, gender, ability, disability, inclusion, and exclusion can directly impact some teachers' ability to create democratic communities. This means that early childhood teachers must look deeper into the ways that power relationships play out in classrooms, for both teachers and children. Unjust treatment of students is unacceptable in a democratic learning community, just as it is unacceptable in a larger democratic society. Kevin's class (like the United States) will not become a united community (a collective *we*) as long as individuals fail to grant every student (and every citizen) full and equal membership and agency. To become a truly democratic learning community (and country), we must deliberate together as fellow travelers. All voices must be heard, valued, and respected before we can begin to define "Who are we?" and "What is our purpose?" as a class, a community, a country. Only then can we fulfill the claim to achieve social justice for everyone.

to achieve one of four basic purposes: to plan and make decisions, to check in, to solve problems, or to raise awareness.

In the case of Kevin's experience, his second grade teacher dismissed his feelings, concerns, and beliefs about how she treated children of color (African American and Hispanic). A more reflective, democratic practitioner would have valued Kevin's feelings and perhaps encouraged him to call a group problem-solving meeting to discuss his concerns about the teacher's response to his request to sharpen his pencil and how it made him feel. This discussion could in turn lead to a broader examination (consciousness-raising aspect) of how different groups of children (across race) feel as a result of these kinds of differential teacher responses. Following five basic steps, a problem-solving class meeting based on Kevin's dilemma could look something like the scenario that follows. (This is a best-case scenario, and not all class meetings and discussions will flow as smoothly.)

Define the Problem

Kevin states (verbally or in writing): "Yesterday, I needed to sharpen my pencil. I saw Dylan, Remi, Kimberly, and Shaila [White boys and girls] get out of their seats to sharpen their pencils. When I asked to sharpen my pencil, I was told to sit down. That's not fair. It made me angry and I didn't like it."

Generate Possible Solutions

Children take turns brainstorming possible solutions.

Kevin: I think everyone should be allowed to sharpen their pencil whenever the point breaks. It's not fair when I see some people sharpening their pencils and I don't get to sharpen mine. Everyone needs to be treated the same.

Dylan: Kevin's right. We all need to sharpen our pencils when they break.

Remi: You can't do your work without a sharpened pencil. If only some of us are allowed to sharpen our pencils, that's not fair. Our class could make a pencil bank with two baskets, one with sharpened pencils and one with unsharpened pencils. Every time someone breaks a pencil, they place it in the unsharpened pencil basket and take a sharpened pencil.

Kimberly: Whenever people break a pencil point, they tell the teacher. That student can ask to sharpen anyone else's pencil as well.

Shaila: Kevin can't get his work done with a broken pencil. If he doesn't get his work done, he gets in trouble. That is not fair to Kevin. We could create a class job. Every week, we have someone who will sharpen all the unsharpened pencils. Each week, a student's name is drawn to do the job. Everyone gets a chance to do the job.

Discuss Solutions

The teacher encourages the children to tell what they think and how they feel about the possible solutions. It is important to extend children's thinking about the nature and consequences for each proposed solution.

At this juncture, an authentically reflective practitioner confronts and reexamines her treatment of individual children and how that treatment impacts all children in the learning community, individually and collectively (see "Reflective Practitioners" on page 102).

Reach Consensus

Reaching consensus on decisions or solutions can be the most challenging aspect of class meetings. Fulfilling a deliberative process in which all voices are heard is as important as the final decision itself. In this instance, the children would need to decide what is most important: the act of sharpening or having access to a sharpened pencil.

Kevin states, "If I raise my hand with a broken pencil, I need to either sharpen it or get a pencil that is sharpened." Everyone agrees.

The class could decide to combine solutions. They could create a pencil bank and appoint a pencil banker whose weekly job is to maintain the pencil supply. Anyone who needs a

Reflection Questions

These questions provide an opportunity for critical reflection and analysis about self-identity and agency in young children. They also encourage discussions about the importance of reflective practices that further support democratic learning communities for young children.

1. How did the second grade teacher's deficit thinking impact the classroom community as a whole?

2. What kinds of knowledge, skills, and dispositions do reflective practitioners need to create and manage positive democratic learning communities that grant full membership to all children?

3. When teachers fail to reflect on their classroom practices, what are the potential outcomes for teaching and learning?

4. How do the culturally responsive practices described and illustrated in the article promote young children's self-identity, agency, and sense of community?

5. How do teacher–student interactions impact families and communities beyond the classroom setting?

sharpened pencil raises her hand with the broken pencil, and the teacher will let everyone replace their pencil with a sharpened pencil. Everyone has equal access to the sharpened pencils. When there is only one remaining pencil in the basket, the banker sharpens all the broken pencils.

Evaluate

At a later time, the class can revisit how well the pencil bank is working. The teacher and students can ask, "Does everyone have equal access? Is there anything we can do to improve the system? Has it created any problems we need to resolve?"

Conclusion

Kevin's classroom dilemma and what it means for his self-identity and agency is part of an emerging set of discourses about children that recognize them as active citizens with rights (Corsaro 2014; Mayall 2013), as competent beings (Smith, Duncan, & Marshall 2005), and as having unique voices and the ability to shape their own identities and create their social worlds (Christensen & Prout 2005; Greene & Hill 2005). It is important that such practices be understood as fundamental to the design, creation, and implementation of early childhood curricula and learning environments. Kevin is now a young man, and his mother reminds him to this day, "We are many members, but one body."

References

Barbarin, O. 2010. "Halting African American Boys' Progression From Pre-K to Prison: What Families, Schools, and Communities Can Do!" *American Journal of Orthopsychiatry* 80 (1): 81–88.

Barbarin, O. 2013. "A Longitudinal Examination of Socioemotional Learning in African American and Latino Boys Across the Transition From Pre-K to Kindergarten." *American Journal of Orthopsychiatry* 83 (2–3): 156–64.

Barbarin, O., & G.M. Crawford. 2006. "Acknowledging and Reducing Stigmatization of African American Boys." *Young Children* 61 (6): 79–86.

Bishop, R.S. 1990. "Mirrors, Windows, and Sliding Glass Doors." *Perspectives: Choosing and Using Books for the Classroom* 6 (3): ix–xi.

Christensen, P., & A. Prout. 2005. "Anthropological and Sociological Perspectives on the Study of Children." Chap. 3 in *Researching Children's Experience: Approaches and Methods,* eds. S. Greene & D. Hogan. London: Sage.

Corsaro, W.A. 2014. *The Sociology of Childhood.* 4th ed. Sociology for a New Century series. Thousand Oaks, CA: Sage.

Davis, J.E. 2005. "Early Schooling and Academic Achievement of African American Males." Chap. 5 in *Educating African American Males: Voices From the Field,* ed. O.S. Fashola. Thousand Oaks, CA: Corwin.

Derman-Sparks, L., & J.O. Edwards. 2010. *Anti-Bias Education for Young Children and Ourselves.* Washington, DC: NAEYC.

DeVries, R., & C. Sales. 2011. *Ramps and Pathways: A Constructivist Approach to Physics With Young Children.* Washington, DC: NAEYC.

DSC (Developmental Studies Center). 1996. *Ways We Want Our Class to Be: Class Meetings That Build Commitment to Kindness and Learning.* Oakland, CA: DSC.

Gangi, J.M. 2004. *Encountering Children's Literature: An Arts Approach.* Boston: Allyn & Bacon.

Greene, S.M., & Hill, M. 2005. "Researching Children's Experience: Methods and Methodological Issues." Chap. 1 in *Researching Children's Experiences: Approaches and Methods,* eds. S.M. Greene and D.M. Hogan. London: Sage.

Hamre, B.K., & R.C. Pianta. 2001. "Early Teacher–Child Relationships and the Trajectory of Children's School Outcomes Through Eighth Grade." *Child Development* 72 (2): 625–38.

Harper, S.R., & Associates. 2014. *Succeeding in the City: A Report From the New York City Black and Latino Male High School Achievement Study.* Philadelphia: Center for the Study of Race and Equity in Education, University of Pennsylvania. www.gse.upenn.edu/equity/sites/gse.upenn.edu.equity/files/publications/Harper_and_Associates_2014.pdf.

Howard, L.C., J.C. Rose, & O.A. Barbarin. 2013. "Raising African American Boys: An Exploration of Gender and Racial Socialization Practices." *American Journal of Orthopsychiatry* 83 (2–3): 218–30.

Kafele, B.K. 2009. *Motivating Black Males to Achieve in School and in Life.* Alexandria, VA: ASCD.

Kohn, A. 2006. *Beyond Discipline: From Compliance to Community.* 2nd ed. Alexandria, VA: ASCD.

Mayall, B. 2013. *A History of the Sociology of Childhood.* London: Institute of Education, University of London.

McNair, J.C. 2014. "'I Didn't Know There Were Black Cowboys': Introducing American Families to African American Children's Literature." *Young Children* 69 (1): 64–69.

Rasinski, T.V. 2010. *The Fluent Reader: Oral and Silent Reading Strategies for Building Fluency, Word Recognition, and Comprehension.* 2nd ed. New York: Scholastic.

Smith, A., J. Duncan, & K. Marshall. 2005. "Children's Perspectives on Their Learning: Exploring Methods." *Early Child Development and Care* 175 (6): 473–87.

Tennessee Department of Education. 2013. "Second Grade: Life in the United States." https://www.tn.gov/assets/entities/education/attachments/std_ss_gr_2.pdf.

Thompson, M.C. 1996. "Mentors on Paper: How Classics Develop Verbal Ability." Chap. 4 in *Developing Verbal Talent: Ideas and Strategies for Teachers of Elementary and Middle Schools Students,* eds. J. VanTassel-Baska, D.T. Johnson, & L.N. Boyce. Boston: Allyn & Bacon.

Urban Art. 2014. "Mural Dedications at Willow Park and at Pine Hill Community Center." www.urbanartcommission.org/news/june-mural-dedications-at-willow-park-and-pinehill-community-center.

Vance, E. 2015. *Class Meetings: Young Children Solving Problems Together.* Rev. ed. Washington, DC: NAEYC.

Wright, B. 2011. "I Know Who I Am, Do You? Identity and Academic Achievement of Successful African American Male Adolescents in an Urban Pilot High School in the United States." *Urban Education* 46 (4): 611–38.

About the Authors

Brian L. Wright, PhD, is an assistant professor of early childhood education in the Department of Instruction and Curriculum Leadership at the University of Memphis, in Tennessee. Brian's research focuses on high-achieving African American males in urban schools pre-K–12, racial–ethnic identity development of boys and young men of color, African American males as early childhood teachers, and teacher identity development.

Shelly L. Counsell, EdD, is an assistant professor of early childhood education in the Department of Instruction and Curriculum Leadership at the University of Memphis. Shelly's research interests include constructivism, inclusion, disability studies, diversity, early STEM, and democratic learning communities.

Shelby L. Tate, MA, is the academic services associate in the Department of Instruction and Curriculum Leadership/Graduate Admissions at the University of Memphis. Shelby is an advisor for the MS, EdS, and EdD programs and was the 2014 Kindle Award Honoree for her dedication and service.

Community Explorers: Critical Thinking Strategies for Supporting Dual Language Learners

Tamara Spencer and Lisa Hertzog

"¿Como ayuda a la gente?" (How do you help people?), first-grader Alexa asks a pharmacist and then attentively records the pharmacist's response. Huddling around the interviewee with clipboards in hand, young reporters inquisitively probe as to the nature of her work, the skills required for this work, and the benefit in helping those who are ill. Much preparation has gone into this field trip, even though the destination is only a block away from school. These young reporters ask *thick questions*—questions that require the speaker to extend beyond a yes-or-no response. The pharmacist fluidly switches between Spanish and English—much like the children do. She enthusiastically answers each question, taking time from her busy workday to share her knowledge and enthusiasm with children from her community.

Dual language learners (DLLs)—children who arrive at school acquiring more than one language—represent one of the fastest growing populations in US public schools (NCES 2014). However, all too often longstanding misconceptions about children's dual language development (Puig 2010) can prevent the use of practices that promote critical thinking among bilingual children. These myths include the

> Assumption that children automatically learn a second language by being in a dual language environment

> Belief that conversational language is the equivalent of academic language

> Misconception that there are limited opportunities to integrate home languages into the everyday curriculum

However, teachers have opportunities to debunk these myths, fostering children's bilingualism and problem-solving skills through experiential and social learning opportunities. In this article, Lisa, a first grade teacher (one of the authors of this article), effectively applies research-based strategies to promote critical thinking practices with young DLLs. She helps the children create a bilingual inquiry community, rich with new ideas and content worthy of exploration and problem solving.

Viewing Bilingualism as a Resource

Critical thinking in early childhood goes hand in hand with oral language development; it is through language and communication that children develop the intellectual disposition to explore new ideas (Genishi & Dyson 2009). Dual language learners' literacy development flourishes in classrooms that provide abundant opportunities to read and write in their home languages and English. Reading and writing informational texts and exploring real-world knowledge give DLLs opportunities to explore and communicate about complex ideas. Teaching vocabulary and grammar in isolation, with an emphasis on language proficiency, can alienate young learners. Instead, teachers can create an environment that positions literacy as a social meaning-making process, a place to explore printed text in a vibrant and diverse linguistic community. When young children's bilingualism is viewed as a resource, educators support instruction that fosters critical thinking, allowing DLLs to grapple with rich content knowledge and broaden their language use and capacities (Falchi, Axelrod, & Genishi 2013; Nieto 2010; Ruíz 1984).

A major principle of dual language learning is that language knowledge transfers: "If a child learns how to read in one language, that child knows how to read, and that general ability will facilitate learning to read in another language" (Krashen 1996, 23). Regardless of language background, teaching children to ask questions and communicate with one another as they encounter new information is central to teaching critical thinking skills (Salmon 2010; Whittaker 2014). Teachers can design curricular tasks worthy of deep exploration even when children are learning more than one language.

Tapping into the children's *funds of knowledge*—the accumulation of a child's cultural, linguistic, and historic background knowledge (González, Moll, & Amanti 2005)—can uncover new ways to promote children's critical thinking and inquiry. Teachers can build on children's prior knowledge and primary language experiences, creating new opportunities for rich, purposeful engagement with language and literacy. Young children tend to communicate more readily in social environments that effectively build on their funds of knowledge. For example, children who regularly take public transit might be well versed in reading maps, observing patterns and behaviors, reading environmental print, and engaging in language about transportation. Thus, teachers can use children's personal experiences to create opportunities that bring children's everyday practices and knowledge into the classroom.

Using Content to Support Critical Thinking and Literacy Skills

The joint position statement on literacy from the International Reading Association (IRA) (now the International Literacy Association) and NAEYC (1998) states, "Young children especially need to be engaged in experiences that make academic content meaningful and build on prior learning" (2). Therefore, rich and meaningful content in which children feel invested provides the platform for complex thought, reasoning, and discussion. In order to develop critical reading and writing skills, DLLs need environments that provide ample room for them to talk. It is through a learning community that supports and relies on children's oral expression that children are prepared to generate authentic questions. Teaching critical thinking and literacy skills through hands-on experiences in content areas such as science, social studies, and math builds on young children's natural curiosity about the world around them (García & Kleifgen 2010). By attending to multiple content areas, teachers also provide continuity with the types of reading and writing experiences that promote skills required for later success in school. In addition, because dual language learners are learning to listen, think, and communicate in more than one language, they have to work harder than monolingual children to exercise focus and attention. It is important to provide an environment conducive to hearing and learning new speech sounds.

Teachers can help children gain knowledge of unfamiliar content in their home languages as a way to better understand and communicate new ideas in English (Goldenberg 2008). For example, in the opening vignette young children learned to interview a specialist while also developing new vocabulary (in two languages), such as *drugstore/la farmacía*, *prescription/la receta médica*, *patient/el paciente*, and *measure/medir*. Teachers can use multiple methods to convey new concepts—visual, auditory, and textual clues that maximize the child's ability to conceptualize, analyze, and apply new content. In this situation, the teacher and children immediately transformed the dramatic play area into a pharmacy after the field trip, creating a space for the young children to actively rehearse and use related vocabulary they recently learned. Photos and videos of things in the environment that are familiar to the students, captured with a digital camera, can be used to create games and manipulatives to give children a better understanding of the concepts they are learning.

The approach to supporting DLLs' critical thinking and language skills is universal: all young children thrive when teachers

> View them as capable language users

> Build curricula that tap into the children's funds of knowledge

> Develop curricula that allow them to wonder about new information

The Setting

This article showcases Lisa's first grade classroom that supported the development of dual language learners. Lisa, a National Board Certified Teacher, was in her seventh year of teaching. She taught at a dual language school in an urban northeastern city, where instruction alternated between English one day and Spanish the next. The majority of students were from families with low incomes and participated in the federally funded lunch program. Located in a part of the city known for its racial and linguistic diversity, the school's administrators, teachers, students, and families viewed bilingualism as a linguistic asset and necessity in today's global society. Nearly all of the 20 children Lisa taught were Latinos whose families originated largely from the Dominican Republic, Puerto Rico, and Cuba. Most of the children were DLLs, coming from bilingual or Spanish-speaking homes, with various levels of English fluency.

Community Explorers/
Los exploradoros de nuestra comunidad

In early spring, Lisa and the class embarked on a two-month study of the people in the school's neighborhood by visiting and interviewing the employees at the local bike shop/*la tienda de bicicletas*, post office/*la oficina de correos*, food pantry/*la despensa de alimentos*, and drugstore/ *la farmacía* (highlighted in the opening vignette). Drawing on the research of Hong (2001), this social studies curriculum and community inquiry integrated children's language, literacy, and critical thinking skills. The children used knowledge in real-life situations to help them think critically. Focusing on the children's own community offered them an opportunity to step into a familiar adult world, experience the life of their neighborhood, and think about the roles of reading and writing in two languages in everyday interactions. From the time the unit was announced, the children drew on their funds of knowledge to locate themselves and their stories within the context of their community. For example, the children were eager to contribute to a discussion on the school's broader community, noting important landmarks, key individuals, popular parks and meeting areas, and transportation hubs. Relying on their background knowledge, children also mentioned familiar professions like firefighter/ *el bombero* and doctor/*el medico*. By seeking and valuing the children's ideas as an important part of

Digital Documentation Tips

Documenting children's learning with technology is a powerful tool for teachers as they plan and reflect. It offers a framework for both children and teachers to learn how and why learning occurs in order to deepen the meaning of what is studied. Gather digital records of children's projects— photos, quotes, scanned work samples, commentary, and so on—in a repository such as a password-protected blog or electronic journal to help families and children make sense of and build on the learning. Here are some suggestions for documentation.

> Record the process, rather than the product, of children's learning.

> Have children present and engaged with you in the documentation process. Include the children's words as well as your own reflections.

> Ask the children about their processes either while recording or when they're viewing the documentation later.

> Use questions that start with *what* or *how* (What did you learn when you asked your family these questions? How did you decide where to put the school on your map?).

> Ask yourself what is more important to document—for example, the children's words, photographs of the children, or an artifact of the project. As you edit the presentation, check to see that what you and the children value most is clearly visible.

> Ask someone to review your documentation—someone who can edit, get you to think more deeply, and challenge you in positive ways.

From W. Parnell and J. Bartlett, "iDocument: How Smartphones and Tablets Are Changing Documentation in Preschool and Primary Classrooms," *Young Children* 67 (May 2012): 50–56.

the curriculum, Lisa emphasized the depth of their knowledge and the contributions they made to the group's learning while also fostering their dual language learning.

The Process

Field trips provided real-world applications of ideas and created authentic opportunities for children to generate questions and write regularly. To prepare for the trips, the students listed all the questions they wanted to ask the workers. Then they voted for the top six questions. This selection involved much critical thinking as, prior to voting, they categorized the questions, grouped similar questions, and considered which ones would elicit the most information. They also discussed questioning techniques and using thick questions, as illustrated in the opening vignette. These students were learning how to compare questions to distinguish basic ones from those that required inferential and higher-order processing skills. For example, they recognized that questions like "Is your job fun?" provided less detail from the respondent than asking "Why do you like your job?" The children took ownership of the ideas and had a vested interest in seeking out the answers. In the end, these questions focused on employees' career selections and qualifications, job responsibilities, interactions with others, and their lives outside of their jobs. Asking the children to reflect deeply on their questions helped them develop their abstract thinking skills, which transferred across languages.

The following day, they translated their questions into English (as the previous day was taught in Spanish) so they could communicate with all the community members, many of whom were bilingual. Lisa created a two-sided handout with the questions—one side in Spanish and the other English—and the children used the template throughout the unit. The handouts provided a model for asking questions and promoting thinking and inquiry skills. Regardless of the target language for the day's lesson, students still had (a) the means to fully participate in the learning activity, (b) a template for asking questions in both languages, and (c) a tool to extend their thinking through the duration of the study.

Building on the Children's and the Community's Funds of Knowledge

As they took on the role of researchers, the first-graders built on their cultural and linguistic knowledge—as well as the community's—as they had authentic purposes for speaking, listening, reading, and writing. To practice interviewing, children selected family members to interview in the language of their choice. Posing the questions to an adult with whom they had a warm relationship helped the children comfortably practice the tone, fluency, and demeanor needed to later engage in a more formal interview. Throughout this study, the day would begin or end with the children reading aloud their findings about their family members' careers, which affirmed the diversity of careers represented in the families of the class. For example, Rafaela shared that her mother worked as a hospital administrator; Kenny proudly explained that his father drove a bus around the city; and Luisa said that her mother taught third grade at a school down the street. Sharing their interview results with one another, the children extended, elaborated on, and revised their initial understanding of conducting interviews and becoming researchers.

In the next part of the study, Lisa and the class ventured out to visit local businesses and witness the expertise of the community members. The investigation began with a visit to

Julio's Bike Shop. Many students pass the shop on their way to and from school and had admired the new bicycles displayed in the window. As they interviewed Manuel, one of Julio's employees, the children were surprised to learn that the bike shop was not only a place to buy a new bike but also where they could bring a bike that needed repair. They were fascinated as Manuel showed them a bike chain he was replacing during the visit. These first-graders learned that Manuel's job responsibilities included both fixing bicycles and tending the store's counter.

This curriculum honored the children's and the community's bilingualism, as many of the field trips used Spanish and English. The first-graders observed that many people in the community were bilingual, with a large population having immigrated from the Dominican Republic and other Spanish-speaking countries. In the community, the children easily switched to the language most comfortable to the person they were interviewing. As a result, their bilingualism emerged through authentic interactions, providing an opportunity to pick up on linguistic cues when communicating with new people. For example, in discussions they noted intonation, body language, and follow-up questioning as valuable ways to enhance conversations. Their bilingualism became a source of pride, a resource they relied on to represent new and evolving ideas about the community and the people in it.

Reading and Writing in Two Languages

The children's literacy development flourished due to their abundant opportunities to read and write in both languages (see "Select English and Spanish Children's Literature" on page 112). Through the alternating daily instruction in Spanish and English, they learned complex content in their home language and transferred that knowledge to English. For example, in the post office visit, Lisa and the students followed the process

Select English and Spanish Children's Literature

> *Bus Drivers/Conductores de autobuses* (2010), by Jacqueline Laks Gorman

> *A Day in the Life of a Builder* (2001), by Linda Hayward

> *Jobs Around My Neighborhood/Oficios en mi vecindario* (2002), by Gladys Rosa-Mendoza

> *Los bomberos (Personas de la comunidad/People in the community)* (2008), by Diyan Leake

> *The Post Office Book: Mail and How It Moves* (1986), by Gail Gibbons

> *Un dia en la vida de un bombero* (2006), by Linda Hayward

of mailing a letter: writing a letter, buying a stamp, placing the letter in the mailbox, following it through the sorting process, and finally seeing the letter make it to the mailroom where mail carriers took it in their wheeled bags to its final destination. Later, Lisa and the children charted this process in a flowchart, first in Spanish and the following day in English. Through this process they created a chart of critical vocabulary words (in Spanish and in English) that served as a visual resource for children who were dominant in one language. The vocabulary that emerged through the field trips demonstrated how *cognates*—words with common origins—provide a powerful way for children to use their knowledge in both languages. For example, the Spanish verbs for *sort*—*clasificar* and *ordenar*—helped them know the English words *classify* and *put in order*.

Offering Children Choices

In preparation for the last field trip of the unit, each child selected a primary focus for the drugstore investigation—interviewing the store manager or pharmacist, making a list of the items in the store, or drawing a map of the store. Providing choices allowed the children to reflect on the ideas they were interested in and take ownership of their learning. Since DLLs benefit from teachers modeling linguistic and problem-solving processes, Lisa began by working with the children who had chosen to draw a map of the store. She encouraged them to draw it from a bird's-eye view, imagining that they were flying high above the store. Lisa introduced spatial reasoning—a complex and critical skill—at the beginning of the unit by having the children build a model of the classroom with blocks. Now the children could expand on this logic, applying and transferring their knowledge of mapping to a new scenario.

Conclusion

The children understood that they were members of a community of inquiry. After each of the field trips, the students returned to the classroom to report back on all that they had discovered. Gathering on the rug, each group reported their findings to the class as the other children added to their notes. Throughout the neighborhood investigations, the children wondered at the diversity of the careers, products, and services available in the surrounding community.

The Community Explorers unit was based on the assumption that *all* young children—including dual language learners—thrive when provided with a learning environment where they can ponder and question while experiencing a creative, complex, and developmentally appropriate approach to early literacy. Lisa built on the children's natural curiosity while also prompting them to think critically by engaging them in purposeful activities and learning experiences. As a result, these young children took ownership of their learning and developed the intellectual dispositions to reflect on and grapple with new information in two languages, thus increasing fluency in both.

References

Falchi, L.T., Y. Axelrod, & C. Genishi. 2013. "'Miguel es un artista'—and Luisa Is an Excellent Student: Seeking Time and Space for Children's Multimodal Practices." *Journal of Early Childhood Literacy* 14 (3): 345–66.

García, O., & J. Kleifgen. 2010. *Educating Emergent Bilinguals. Policies, Programs, and Practices for English Language Learners.* New York: Teachers College Press.

Genishi, C., & A.H. Dyson. 2009. *Children, Language, and Literacy: Diverse Learners in Diverse Times.* New York: Teachers College Press; Washington, DC: NAEYC.

Goldenberg, C. 2008. "Teaching English Language Learners: What the Research Does—and Does Not—Say." *American Educator* 32: 8–23, 42–44. www.aft.org/pdfs/americaneducator/summer2008/goldenberg.pdf.

González, N., L.C. Moll, & C. Amanti, eds. 2005. *Funds of Knowledge: Theorizing Practices in Households, Communities, and Classrooms.* Mahwah, NJ: Erlbaum.

Hong, M. 2001. *Teaching First Grade: A Practical Guide. A Mentor Teacher Shares Insights, Strategies, and Lessons for Teaching Reading, Writing, and Math—and Laying the Foundation for Learning Success.* New York: Scholastic.

IRA (International Reading Association) & NAEYC. 1998. "Learning to Read and Write: Developmentally Appropriate Practices for Young Children." Joint position statement. www.naeyc.org/files/naeyc/file/positions/PSREAD98.PDF.

Krashen, S.D. 1996. *Under Attack: The Case Against Bilingual Education.* Culver City, CA: Language Education Associates.

NCES (National Center for Educational Statistics). 2014. "English Language Learners." *The Condition of Education.* Washington, DC: US Department of Education. http://nces.ed.gov/programs/coe/indicator_cgf.asp.

Nieto, S. 2010. *Language, Culture, and Teaching: Critical Perspectives.* 2nd ed. New York: Routledge.

Puig, V.I. 2010. "Are Early Intervention Services Placing Home Languages and Cultures 'At Risk'?" *Early Childhood Research and Practice* 12 (1). http://ecrp.uiuc.edu/v12n1/puig.html.

Ruíz, R. 1984. "Orientations in Language Planning." *NABE: The Journal for the National Association of Bilingual Education* 8 (2): 15–34.

Salmon, A.K. 2010. "Tools to Enhance Young Children's Thinking." *Young Children* 65 (5): 26–31. www.naeyc.org/tyc/files/tyc/file/V4N5/Tools%20to%20Enhance%20Young%20CHildren's%20Thinking.pdf.

Whittaker, J.V. 2014. "Good Thinking! Fostering Children's Reasoning and Problem Solving." Research in Review. *Young Children* 69 (3): 80–89. www.naeyc.org/yc/article/fostering_childrens_reasoning_whittaker.

About the Authors

Tamara Spencer, EdD, is assistant professor and program director for the Teachers for Tomorrow program at Saint Mary's College in Moraga, California. Her research analyzes the intersections of curricula and young children's multimodal and multilingual literacy practices. In addition, she has taught in K–3 public schools in Philadelphia and New York.

Lisa Hertzog, EdD, is executive director of teacher effectiveness for the New York City Department of Education.

Lessons Learned From a Teacher Working With Culturally and Linguistically Diverse Children

Carla Amaro-Jiménez

"Mrs. Pennington always wanted me to show her—you know, explain my thinking. This is why I like her so much, and what I liked the most about being in third grade."

—Diego, final interview

Classroom demographics are rapidly changing. Not only are primary classrooms more culturally diverse, the number of home languages (languages other than English) spoken by children and their families is increasing every year. While the percentage of school-age children considered culturally and linguistically diverse (CLD) is 45.7 percent (NCES 2013), such students will become the majority in schools by 2030, if not sooner (Hussar & Bailey 2014; US Census Bureau 2012). However, the teaching workforce is not as diverse as the children in US classrooms—approximately 16 percent of teachers are CLD (NCES 2008).

Cultural and linguistic differences between teachers and students can impact learning and teaching in many ways (NCES 2008). For instance, what would you think if a student refused to look at you when you talked to him, and looked down instead? Is this a sign of disrespect? For children from some cultures, not looking directly at the person speaking is considered respectful. Being aware of and understanding such cultural differences is necessary, because an educator's teaching practices and approach to teaching are related to the school success of students from diverse backgrounds and cultures (Bohon, MacPherson, & Atiles 2005). Learning from the experiences of teachers who work with students who are CLD is valuable for helping teachers increase all children's academic achievement (Derman-Sparks & Edwards 2010). Strategies these teachers use can help others learn about how to meet the needs of dual language learners, as well as those of students of various ethnicities and with other unique backgrounds.

This article describes some of the practices I learned from Mrs. Pennington, a teacher I got to know well when I was an active participant and observer in her classroom for a year. During that year, I saw firsthand what teachers whose background and life experiences differ from those of their students can do to ensure all children learn, particularly culturally and linguistically diverse children (Amaro-Jiménez 2008). I highlight the ways in which her instruction addresses the needs of such students through five lessons learned.

1. Give children time to think and reflect in their own way.

2. Encourage students to value what they know.

3. Help students to incorporate their peers' experiences into their own knowledge.

4. Take the time to listen, and do so carefully.

5. Help children connect new and existing information to understand new knowledge.

Getting to Know Mrs. Pennington

The day I meet Mrs. Pennington (not her real name), a third grade teacher at an urban Title I elementary school in the Midwest, I am struck with mixed emotions. On the one hand, there are visible economic and social challenges present in the community that make me wonder what is happening inside the tall, brick walls surrounding the school. I mistakenly assume Mrs. Pennington is overwhelmed with economic, social, and academic challenges in her classroom and school community. However, walking the school's hallways and seeing how well the school is maintained shows that people at this school care about every child here. As I speak to her, I learn that she is aware of the challenges confronted by the families who live in the neighborhood and the role poverty can play as a deterrent to achievement. She also acknowledges that despite these circumstances she has high expectations for all of the children. She believes families have a vital role in their children's learning. She talks about engaging families, not just involving them in school events.

Mrs. Pennington taught at a predominantly white, middle-class school for three years before working at this school. While she is well versed in research and how it informs her practice, when she first started working here she knew only "the basics of working and meeting the needs of students with culturally and linguistically diverse backgrounds." She indicates that the demographics in her classroom are significantly different from other schools where she has taught, and that initially she was not sure whether she would be an effective teacher.

Prior to teaching at her current school, she had always known what to do and what to expect from the students. She knew she would need to rethink which teaching practices would meet these students' diverse needs.

Seven of the 23 students in Mrs. Pennington's class are African American, two are Asian, one is Middle Eastern, nine are Caucasian, and four are Latino. But diversity goes beyond ethnicity in this classroom. Two are children of migrant workers and five are dual language learners. Seven have individualized education plans (IEPs) because of hearing and/or speech delays or impairments, and the dual language learners also have IEPs as directed by their district policy to ensure various school personnel are accommodating their needs and ensuring their progress. Three of the children are bused to a gifted and talented program in the district for the last two hours of the school day. All children qualify for free or reduced-price lunch.

Even though all the children are considered by the school as being at-risk, Mrs. Pennington works to ensure each has the opportunity to succeed. She knows she has to tap into the children's and their families' *funds of knowledge* (González, Moll, & Amanti 2005)—their unique lived and cultural experiences—to make her teaching meaningful for all. "So how do you meet the needs of all these students? Do you have different goals for each of them?" I ask. She explains, "It is not about setting particular goals for this group and other goals for that group. All of them are mine. I need to look out for *all of them*" (Amaro-Jiménez 2008, 186). As I sit in the classroom, I pay close attention to the ways in which she gives all the students opportunities to learn and to become part of this diverse classroom—a community of children with different interests, abilities, backgrounds, and needs, but with one thing in common: the desire to have the opportunity to succeed academically, one lesson at a time.

Lesson 1: Give Children Time to Think and Reflect in Their Own Way

In this accountability era, teachers often feel pressured to go from one standard to the next, trying to ensure that students master what they need to know before moving on to another concept (Stillman 2009). It can be hard to find time to offer children opportunities to slow down and think—to reflect and go beyond what the curriculum prescribes. With effort, Mrs. Pennington has made thinking and reflection an integral part of her daily instruction. As a result, the students can think about what they have learned previously, reflect on what that learning means to them, and begin gathering their thoughts about what they are going to learn (Bransford, Brown, & Cocking 2000).

Her lessons begin with the announcement, "It's thinking time!" Whenever students hear that, they put on their thinking caps (each child has made a hat out of construction paper) and begin thinking. After writing the topic of that day or week on a whiteboard, Mrs. Pennington draws the students' attention to the Big Qs—three questions she always asks either before introducing a topic or as they begin working on a lesson related to a topic they have already discussed. For instance, at the start of a review lesson about habitats, she asks the following Big Qs: "What does the word *habitat* remind you of?," "What have you learned about habitats already?," and "What are examples of habitats?"

Thinking time varies depending on how familiar the students are with the topic. Mrs. Pennington reserves between three and five minutes for thinking time during each lesson. Because the three questions are ones she often asks and are permanently displayed on the

whiteboard, children know what to expect beforehand. Having a list of questions before the lesson that they are expected to answer is particularly beneficial for the students who are culturally and linguistically diverse. Some have been attending US public schools for only a few years (or even months) and are still learning classroom dynamics. Also, because she knows most of her students struggle with English vocabulary, she writes key words related to the concept on a chart that is visible to all and encourages students to use the words when they share their thoughts during thinking time.

When the topics are more challenging, Mrs. Pennington gives the students extra thinking time and encourages them to tap into their funds of knowledge. Making use of these resources is important, given that the students are motivated to draw on what they learn at home from their immediate and extended families (Amaro-Jiménez & Semingson 2010; Heath 1983). For instance, when reviewing what they had learned about habitats, she asks the students to think of specific habitats they may have seen or heard about at home (e.g., "Where does your pet live—indoors or outdoors?") and about their home culture as it relates to the topic (e.g., "Do people in your family have birds as pets?").

Even though Mrs. Pennington speaks only English, the children know they can use their home language as part of their learning. She encourages students to write in their home language along with English, especially when they know cognates (i.e., words in different languages that resemble one another, such as the English and Spanish words *camouflage/ camuflaje, pelican/pelícano*). It is fascinating to see students write little notes to themselves about what the words mean or how they are said in their home languages. Mrs. Pennington asks the dual language learners about what they have written and what those words mean in their home languages because she wants to learn their languages as well. She often tells the children how important it is for all of them, and for her, to use their "inner resources"— characteristics of themselves and their culture—as part of their learning experience.

Helping Dual Language Learners Acquire Academic Vocabulary

Providing opportunities for students to acquire and use content-area language is critical to their learning success. A good grasp of academic language enables students not only to understand what is being taught in the classroom but also to engage in conversations and follow routines in and out of the classroom. The Common Core State Standards underscore the importance of understanding academic language. Here are a few examples.

Vocabulary Acquisition and Use

CCSS.ELA-LITERACY.CCRA.L.4: Determine or clarify the meaning of unknown and multiple-meaning words and phrases by using context clues, analyzing meaningful word parts, and consulting general and specialized reference materials, as appropriate.

Craft and Structure

CCSS.ELA-LITERACY.CCRA.R.4: Interpret words and phrases as they are used in a text, including determining technical, connotative, and figurative meanings, and analyze how specific word choices shape meaning or tone.

CCSS.ELA-LITERACY.RI.3.4: Determine the meaning of general academic and domain-specific words and phrases in a text relevant to a . . . topic or subject area. (NGA & CCSSO 2010)

Teaching the language of the content areas in ways that are responsive to all students' experiences and levels of language proficiency is necessary. Keep in mind that some dual language learners may already have some content knowledge and academic vocabulary in their home language; others are developing this knowledge and vocabulary in school, either in English only or in English and their home language. Having prior knowledge in their home language can facilitate the transfer of both concepts and vocabulary more easily into students' second language (Ovando & Combs 2012), so tap into students' rich cultural and linguistic resources.

Below are some strategies for supporting students' acquisition of academic vocabulary. Academic language learning is likely a lifelong process, so students need opportunities to learn and use words meaningfully.

> **Cognates.** Students who have acquired some academic concepts in their home language may be familiar with some of the vocabulary already. Making use of cognates, which are words that have similar spellings and meanings in more than one language,

can aid students' language learning. Some examples of English/Spanish cognates include gallon/galón, important/importante, and planet/planeta. (A very helpful list is at www.colorincolorado.org/sites/default/files/Cognate-List.pdf.) Note that there are also false cognates—words that look similar in both languages but have different meanings—such as the words exit/éxito (translates to "success") and idiom/idioma (translates to "language").

> **Visual scaffolds.** Find ways to visually display the academic language students are learning. For instance, a Frayer model is a graphic organizer that can help students identify basic information about a vocabulary word. Students write a word they are studying (e.g., valley) in a box that is attached to four larger boxes. The content of the other boxes may include a definition of the word (e.g., "a low land area"), examples and non-examples (e.g., example: "Sonoma Valley"; non-example: "Mount Everest"), a sentence that includes the word (e.g., "The Sonoma Valley is located in California"), the part of speech it represents (e.g., noun), and even an illustration. Other visual scaffolds include adding synonyms to word walls and creating a visual dictionary students use for classroom work.

> **Student pairs.** Students need opportunities to use their new academic language in multiple settings and contexts (e.g., a science experiment, physical education; group work, individual work). Make an explicit effort to use this language and make it part of everyday interactions. A simple but effective strategy is to have students work in pairs to practice and discuss the vocabulary they are learning. For instance, students might describe to their partners, in their own words, what they understood about a vocabulary term and then create a shared definition for it. Pairs could also act out a term for everyone else to identify or as they practice their lines for a Readers Theater activity.

References

NGA (National Governors Association) & CCSSO (Council of Chief State School Officers). 2010. "English Language Arts Standards." www.corestandards.org/ELA-Literacy.

Ovando, C.J., & M.C. Combs. 2012. *Bilingual and ESL Classrooms: Teaching in Multicultural Contexts.* 5th ed. New York: McGraw-Hill.

Lesson 2: Encourage Students to Value What They Know

Student participation in Mrs. Pennington's classroom is important. She expects children to listen to one another and to contribute to the discussion. Having a voice in the classroom is important for the dual language learners because this gives them an opportunity to speak out in a supportive environment. Mrs. Pennington does not force students to participate, but they know that participating in classroom activities is a classroom rule. They also know they have to make good use of their thinking time to be able to participate. She often refers to this block of time as their "let's pull our knowledge together" time. It does not matter if the information the children share is completely accurate or not. She emphasizes that it is not the answer she is concerned with, but the ideas that lead them to that answer. Mrs. Pennington's verbal prompts and her small banner over the chalkboard that reads "Our ideas are important!" are daily reminders that it is okay to share ideas—no matter how big or small.

Valuing what they already know about a topic is a cornerstone of her teaching. During a weeklong lesson on developing purpose for reading as well as reading different types of text, she asks them to explain what the word *purpose* means. Karim replies, "Something you do," and Chloe says, "A reason to do something." Mrs. Pennington then builds on Chloe's explanation and asks the children why they read. Several children answer, "Because I like to read" and "Because my mom says it's important." She then asks them to give examples of when and where they read when they are at home. Alejandra says she reads before going to bed, and Thomas says he reads to his little sister because she doesn't know how to read. Manuel says, "I read in the kitchen when my *abuela* [grandmother] is making dinner." Mrs. Pennington asks Manuel to tell the other children what the word *abuela* means, and she asks them if they read with their grandmothers or other family members.

As the children share their thoughts, Mrs. Pennington writes the main points of the discussion on the board, adding the names of those who contribute to the discussion. She feels that it is important for the students to know who is contributing to their own learning and whose ideas they are using to learn about new things. Doing so helps legitimize the

children's ideas, makes them value all the contributions, and highlights the importance of using their inner resources in their learning.

Lesson 3: Help Students to Incorporate Their Peers' Experiences into Their Own Knowledge

Creating a nurturing and caring classroom community is essential when working with children who are culturally and linguistically diverse (Amaro-Jiménez 2012; Moll & González 2004). Mrs. Pennington's students understand they need to rely not only on what they know to complete the classroom tasks, but also on what others know to make learning meaningful. She encourages the students to draw on others' experiences and incorporate them into their classwork. For example, one December morning the children are discussing holidays and how different cultures celebrate them. Juan says his family always makes tamales in December and they "will eat a bunch of them" for Christmas and New Year's. When Mrs. Pennington asks what other children eat for different holidays, Ling talks about the special dumplings her family cooks. She explains the significance of the red lanterns that decorate her home, and why the color red is important to her family and culture.

Later that day, the children write in their journals about what they have learned about various holidays and discuss what they have written. I can hear how they incorporate each others' comments in their writings. Having the opportunity to share and explain their experiences to others, exploring similarities and differences, gives them an appreciation for others' experiences and enables students to use them as part of their own learning (Bransford, Brown, & Cocking 2000).

Lesson 4: Take the Time to Listen, and Do So Carefully

Mrs. Pennington checks to see if students need additional time to work on their activities, if they have any questions, and if they need additional support to understand the topic. With every lesson, she takes a 10-minute walk around the classroom—going to each table to ask open-ended questions (e.g., "Why can we fit this many cubes into this one cube?") and close-ended questions (e.g., "How many cubes fit into this cube?").

Listening carefully to the students is instrumental in Mrs. Pennington's teaching, as evidenced during an activity on symmetry. Alejandra struggles to explain how she has arrived at an answer. Because she at times asks others for answers instead of coming up with her own, Mrs. Pennington knows she needs to check with Alejandra about her understanding. She asks Alejandra to show an example of a symmetrical figure in the handout in front of her. After Alejandra points to several without success, Mrs. Pennington asks her to cut out three of the figures. They then fold these in half to determine which are symmetrical and talk about the rules they discussed earlier in the day for determining whether objects are (or are not) symmetrical. Mrs. Pennington asks Alejandra to write down a rule for identifying symmetrical figures and to revisit her answer.

Mrs. Pennington assesses the students' learning formatively; that is, she does not wait for a lesson to be completed to assess their understanding. She assesses what they are learning in the moment. Doing so helps her determine whether a student needs extra support or additional activities, as in Alejandra's case. Toward the end of her 10-minute walk, Mrs. Pennington jots down the ideas the children share and their questions. She later uses this

Example of a W²HE			
What I learned	**W**here I learned the information	**H**ow I will use this information	**E**xample of how I used this information
■ I learned why recycling is important ■ I know how we can keep our community clean by recycling	■ When we read the book in class ■ Juan's story about the litter in his neighborhood	■ I want to recycle at home ■ We are going to recycle everything in the classroom ■ To do my homework!	■ I recycled plastic and cans at home ■ I used this information to finish my homework

information to help them connect what they have learned with what they are going to learn next, as can be seen in lesson 5.

Lesson 5: Help Children Connect New and Existing Information to Understand New Knowledge

Most teachers are familiar with **KWL** charts. They help us identify what students **K**now about a topic, what they **W**ant to know about it, and what they have **L**earned after instruction ends. Mrs. Pennington uses a strategy beyond typical **KWL** charts; students have opportunities to critically reflect on what they learn, where they learned it, and how they plan to use it, and to give an example. Because the information they each draw on to create the chart results from a collective effort—ideas that everyone shares in class—Mrs. Pennington often refers to the chart as *We* (W²HE) (Amaro-Jiménez 2008). (See "Example of a W²HE.")

Whenever students take part in a We activity, they connect their collective prior experiences with what they are learning. They understand that learning is a shared activity—to master new knowledge, they draw from their own efforts and from their peers' efforts. They learn about their peers' cultures and experiences, and reflect on their own lives. All of these learning efforts are valued in Mrs. Pennington's classroom and provide the children with opportunities to learn in meaningful and multiple ways.

A Final Word on Working With Diverse Learners

Working in a classroom in which children have different home languages, interests, skills, and needs can be difficult for new and seasoned teachers alike. But when we take the time to get to know students' individual characteristics, and when we introduce classroom activities that take these factors into account, learning—and consequently teaching—becomes more meaningful. For Mrs. Pennington's students, learning in her classroom becomes not only a meaningful activity, but a valued one. The third-graders know that she is there to support them, their learning, and their thinking. Diego's comment that explaining his thinking is what he liked "the most about being in third grade" speaks to how valued he felt his ideas were.

When teachers get to know students, identify what students know, and use that information in their instruction (Lee & Bowen 2006), children like Diego will be empowered to use their funds of knowledge and those of others to extend their own understandings. More children will see the classroom as a place where their life experiences, home languages, and diverse cultures are assets, not roadblocks, to learning.

References

Amaro-Jiménez, C. 2008. "Latino Children's English as a Second Language and Subject-Matter Appropriation Through Technology-Mediated Activities: A Cultural Historical Activity Theory Perspective." Electronic doctoral dissertation. University of Cincinnati. https://etd.ohiolink.edu/!etd.send_file?accession=ucin1211 938498&disposition=inline.

Amaro-Jiménez, C. 2012. "Service Learning: Preparing Teachers to Understand Better Culturally and Linguistically Diverse Learners." *Journal of Education for Teaching: International Research and Pedagogy* 38 (2): 211–13.

Amaro-Jiménez, C., & P. Semingson. 2010. "'Sometimes I Don't Know How to Help You, but I'll Try': Latina Mothers' Participation in Their Children's Biliteracy Learning in the Home." *National Journal of Urban Education and Practice* 4 (2): 33–48. www.uta.edu/faculty/carlaaj/docs/NJUEP_Article 3.pdf.

Bohon, S.A., H. MacPherson, & J.H. Atiles. 2005. "Educational Barriers for New Latinos in Georgia." *Journal of Latinos and Education* 4 (1): 43–58.

Bransford, J.D., A.L. Brown, & R.R. Cocking, eds. 2000. *How People Learn: Brain, Mind, Experience, and School.* Expanded ed. Washington, DC: National Academy Press. www.nap.edu/openbook.php?isbn=0309070368.

Derman-Sparks, L., & J.O. Edwards. 2010. *Anti-Bias Education for Young Children and Ourselves.* Washington, DC: NAEYC.

González, N., L.C. Moll, & C. Amanti, eds. 2005. *Funds of Knowledge: Theorizing Practices in Households, Communities, and Classrooms.* New York: Routledge.

Heath, S.B. 1983. *Ways With Words: Language, Life, and Work in Communities and Classrooms.* New York: Cambridge University Press.

Hussar, W.J., & T.M. Bailey 2014. "Projections of Education Statistics to 2022" (NCES 2014-051). National Center for Education Statistics, US Department of Education. Washington, DC: US Government Printing Office.

Lee, J.-S., & N.K. Bowen. 2006. "Parent Involvement, Cultural Capital, and the Achievement Gap Among Elementary School Children." *American Educational Research Journal* 43 (2): 193–218.

Moll, L.C., & N. González. 2004. "Engaging Life: A Funds-of-Knowledge Approach to Multicultural Education." In *Handbook of Research on Multicultural Education,* 2nd ed., eds. J.A. Banks & C.M. Banks, 699–715. San Francisco: Jossey-Bass.

NGA (National Governors Association) & CCSSO (Council of Chief State School Officers). 2010. "English Language Arts Standards." www.corestandards.org/ELA-Literacy.

NCES (National Center for Education Statistics). 2008. "Schools and Staffing Survey (SASS): Percentage Distribution of Public School Teachers, by Race/Ethnicity and State: 2007–08." http://nces.ed.gov/surveys/sass/tables/sass0708_2009324_t1s_02.asp.

NCES. 2013. "Characteristics of Public and Private Elementary and Secondary Schools in the United States: Results From the 2011–12 Schools and Staffing Survey." http://nces.ed.gov/pubs2013/2013312.pdf.

Ovando, C.J., & M.C. Combs. 2012. *Bilingual and ESL Classrooms: Teaching in Multicultural Contexts.* 5th ed. New York: McGraw-Hill.

Stillman, J. 2009. "Taking Back the Standards: Equity-Minded Teachers' Responses to Accountability-Related Instructional Constraints." *The New Educator* 5 (2): 135–60.

US Census Bureau. 2012. "2012 National Population Projections." www.census.gov/population/projections/data/national/2012.html.

About the Author

Carla Amaro-Jiménez, EdD, is an assistant professor of bilingual and English as a second language education at the University of Texas at Arlington. A former early childhood, bilingual teacher, Carla conducts research on instructional practices that support diverse learners and their families in and out of the classroom.

Teacher-Made Assessments Show Students' Growth

Christine J. Ferguson, Susan K. Green, and Carol A. Marchel

Standards-based teaching assessment packages that come with curricular material and mandated curriculum might cause some to think teacher-made assessments of students' learning are not necessary. Nothing could be further from the truth. Given the demand to prepare increasingly diverse learners to meet curriculum standards, teacher-made assessments are more important than ever. Assessments designed by teachers can be sensitive to even small gains toward standards over time. Such assessments can be administered efficiently and frequently and tailored to each child's needs—all necessary factors for designing developmentally appropriate instruction to support students' development.

Five Assessment Steps

This article describes appropriate and efficient research-based assessment strategies that primary teachers can use to track students' progress. One of the most powerful motivators—for both teachers and students—is concrete evidence of students' progress (Green & Johnson 2009). Tracking

Five Assessment Steps

Step 1: Decide What You Want Students to Know

Step 2: Decide How to Measure Essential Outcomes

Step 3: Organize the Information You Collect

Step 4: Collect Information Across Time

Step 5: Interpret the Assessment Results

progress toward goals can energize learners, giving them direction and motivation (Zimmerman 2011).

We have developed a five-step process to help teachers design developmentally appropriate assessments that meet their needs and help teachers and students see gains in desired learning and skills tied to standards. We illustrate each step with examples from primary classrooms (see "Examples of the Five Assessment Steps," page 125).

Step 1: Decide What You Want Students to Know

The first step is to choose the top priority content from the standards. The selection process involves choosing a representative sample of goals (e.g., use nonstandard units to measure the length of objects) that focus on the big ideas, such as measuring lengths indirectly and iterating length units, which are central to the South Carolina College- and Career-Ready (SCCCR) Standards for Mathematics, Measurement and Data Analysis 1.MDA.2: "Use nonstandard physical models to show the length of an object as the number of same size units of length with no gaps or overlaps" (South Carolina Department of Education 2015b). Try to choose concepts that engage students (McTighe & Wiggins 2012).

You can assess multiple standards in an integrated thematic unit. For example, a unit on measurement can address English language arts (ELA) and mathematics standards. To make the content truly meaningful for young students, encourage them to participate in selecting topics that align with the standards and that incorporate their passions and interests (Ferguson 2001). It is important to build a curriculum on students' prior learning and real-life experiences.

For example, after seeing the first-graders' excitement when the construction crew arrived outside their classroom and began building two additional classrooms at the end of the hall, Mr. Edwards decided to replace a planned unit on rocks and soil with one on measurement. He used the first steps in a **KWL** (what I **K**now/what I **W**ant to know/what I **L**earned) chart to organize the students' current understanding and interests. He challenged their thinking by asking, "What do you want to know about measurement?" He recorded their responses under the **W** on the **KWL** chart. Their responses included the following:

Chris: How long will it take the workers to build the classrooms?

Lola: What kinds of tools do they use?

Maria: How do they cut the wood?

Edwardo: How do they know how long to cut the wood?

Roger: Can we help them?

As the unit on measurement unfolded, Mr. Edwards looked for creative ways to make the South Carolina College- and Career-Ready (SCCCR) Standards for Mathematics come to life using the first-graders' fascination with measurement. One goal was to enhance students' writing skills based on the South Carolina College- and Career-Ready (SCCCR) Standards for English Language Arts (ELA), Meaning, Context, and Craft, MCC.2.1: "Explore print and multimedia sources to write informative/explanatory texts that name a topic, supply facts about the topic, and provide a sense of closure" (South Carolina Department of

Examples of the Five Assessment Steps

Step	First Grade Example	Second Grade Example	Third Grade Example
Step 1: Identifying content	**Standard:** The child will compare the lengths of two objects indirectly by using a third object and represent a number of objects with a written numeral. **Selected content:** Measure the lengths of two objects; compare the lengths of two objects (equal to, longer than, shorter than); count the number of units to 120; write the corresponding numeral for each object length; and use operational skills (addition, subtraction) to solve word problems	**Standard:** The child will understand that the three digits of a three-digit number represent amounts of hundreds, tens, and ones. **Selected content:** Compare two three-digit numbers based on meanings of hundreds, tens, and ones digits using <, =, and > symbols to record the results of comparisons.	**Standard:** The child will demonstrate an understanding of two-dimensional shapes. **Selected content:** Identify the specific attributes of circles: center, radius, circumference, and diameter.
Step 2: Designing and administering measurement	**Performance-based checklist:** The teacher asks children to work individually or in small groups with teacher and uses the checklist to track skill levels.	**Performance-based task:** Using a large foam die, and the whiteboard, the teacher models how to play the Place Value Game. During center time, children work in pairs as they take turns rolling a die three times and recording their three-digit number in the appropriate column (Hundreds, Tens, Ones) on a sheet of paper. Partners continue to play the game for nine more rounds. At the end of the game, they compare each round of numbers and discuss which number is less than, equal to, or greater than the other three-digit number.	**Test:** Show a circle, ask children to label center, radius, circumference, and diameter. Give length of radius, ask children to determine length of diameter.
Step 3: Summarizing efficiently	The teacher assigns 2 points for each performance task listed on the checklist completed accurately, for a total of 10 points, with each item worth 10%.	The teacher assigns 1 point for each correct response, for a total of 10 points, with each point worth 10%.	The teacher assigns 1 point each for locating four parts of circle, 2 points for length of radius, for a total of 6 points, with each point worth 17%.
Step 4: Collecting information across time	■ Pre-assessment (described on p. 129). ■ Daily learning log with mathematics standards checklist of skills performed correctly by child for day's topics: measure the lengths of two objects; compare the lengths of two objects (equal to, longer than, shorter than); count the number of units to 120; write the corresponding numeral for each object length; and use addition and subtraction within 20 to solve word problems. ■ Post-assessment (described on p. 129), but add problem-solving questions (e.g., how many more units long is your foot compared to your partner's foot?).	■ Pre-assessment (described on p. 129). ■ Place Value Game results to determine understanding of place value. ■ Post-assessment (described on p. 129), students will individually complete a place value worksheet that includes an extension of the lesson, on which they are to compare numbers and write the appropriate symbol (<, =, or >) on the line between the two numbers.	■ Pre-assessment (described on p. 129). ■ Exit ticket to determine daily content knowledge gains. ■ Post-assessment (described on p. 129) with extension questions.
Step 5: Interpreting results	Compare scores in percentages for each child pre- and post-assessment. Determine which content children still need to learn and reteach.	Compare scores in percentages for each child pre- and post-assessment. Determine which content children still need to learn and reteach.	Compare scores in percentages for each child pre- and post-assessment. Determine which content children still need to learn and reteach.

Education 2015a). To offer relevant resources for the students' writing, Mr. Edwards visited the school media center and public library and selected factual and fictional books about measurement.

Another goal Mr. Edwards chose was to build on students' knowledge of quantity and numeral relationships based on South Carolina College- and Career-Ready (SCCCR) Standards for Mathematics, Number Sense and Base Ten, 1.NSBT.1: "Count forward by ones to 120 starting at any number" (South Carolina Department of Education 2015b). To make the standards meaningful, he collected scraps of wood from the school construction site and a variety of classroom manipulatives such as Unifix cubes, Color Tiles, Measuring Worms counters, Cuisenaire rods, and Link 'N' Learn links and placed them in the math and manipulatives center for students to explore.

Step 2: Decide How to Measure Essential Outcomes

In this step, simplicity and efficiency are necessary for selecting or creating assessment tools that are developmentally appropriate (NAEYC 2011). The measures should be brief and focus on critical concepts and skills. To ensure you have created assessments to match important content (often called *content validity*), you can list typical steps on the route to mastery of essential skills, which can serve as an observation checklist for each child. This is termed *development of a timeline of progress* or a *learning progression* (Smith et al. 2006).

In the first grade example, Mr. Edwards could design a checklist of the hierarchy of skills, from simplest to most complex, at the first grade level that are directly related to the South Carolina College- and Career-Ready (SCCCR) Standards for English Language Arts (ELA), Language Standard 5: "Demonstrate command of the conventions of standard English grammar and usage when writing and speaking" (South Carolina Department of Education 2015a). You can encourage students to write purposefully about a variety of real-life situations, events, or objects. Use the checklist with these writings to determine students' learning over time. As students create stories, some will use invented spelling to convey their thoughts and ideas, which relates to SCCCR ELA, Language L.5.4: "Spell unknown words phonetically; spell common irregularly spelled, grade-appropriate high-frequency words" (South Carolina Department of Education 2015a), while others "use conventional spelling for words with common spelling patterns" (South Carolina Department of Education 2015a), which relates to SCCCR ELA, Language L.5.3. You can then check writing samples from the students' measurement stories completed during a writing workshop against the progression of skills on the checklist.

For a related math example, during group time the following day, Mr. Edwards read Rolf Myller's *How Big Is a Foot?* to the students. He then shared some of the wood scraps and manipulatives that he planned to place in the math and manipulatives center for exploration. During center time, Mr. Edwards worked with small groups of students at the math and manipulatives center as they used various nonstandard units to measure the scraps of wood. He instructed the students to place the units end to end, without gaps or overlaps, to measure the objects. This concept is a foundational building block for the concept of area in third grade. As students measured the wood, they expanded their knowledge by recording the information in their math journals. During center time

that afternoon, they extended their learning by working with a partner to measure other objects in the classroom, including the door, windows, books, tables, whiteboard, computer screen, and their own feet. Again, they recorded their findings in their math journals, where they drew and labeled pictures of objects they measured and wrote numeric quantities. Measuring the length of an object as a whole number of length units is a good indicator of basic mathematical knowledge of measurement skills addressed by the Measurement and Data standard. In addition, counting the number of nonstandard units to 120 illustrates the acquisition of critical mathematical concepts, such as extending the counting sequence and reading and writing numerals to represent number quantities. Mr. Edwards could create a checklist like the "Mathematics Standards Checklist" (page 128) to measure these skills. The checklist reflects the progression of vital mathematical understandings to assess each child's developmental level and is organized to provide information on the entire class at a glance.

Using measures such as these checklists more than once over time lets you document gains in the critical elements of learning. In addition, assessing students' work during one-on-one writing conferences or during small group discussions provides opportunities for personal dialogue and more informal assessment of progress. This dialogue is critical to assess students' understanding of the material and gains made over time. You can use these sources to tailor the curriculum daily to fit students' *zone of proximal development* (ZPD). Vygotsky ([1930–35] 1978) coined this phrase, referring to the difference between what a child can do independently (without guided instruction) and what the child cannot yet do. That is, the zone indicates what the child can accomplish with help from a more capable peer or adult. You can repeat parts of a simple checklist quickly to see the child's progress and changing ZPD.

Mathematics Standards Checklist

Date:_____

Student's Name	SCCCR 1.MDA.1 Measure the lengths of two objects		SCCCR 1.MDA.2 Compare the lengths of two objects		SCCCR 1.NSBT.1 Count the number of units to 120		SCCCR 1.NSBT.1 Write the corresponding numeral for each object length		SCCCR 1.ATO.1 Use operational skills to solve word problems		Total	Comments
	0	1	0	1	0	1	0	1	0	1		
	0	1	0	1	0	1	0	1	0	1		
	0	1	0	1	0	1	0	1	0	1		
	0	1	0	1	0	1	0	1	0	1		
	0	1	0	1	0	1	0	1	0	1		
	0	1	0	1	0	1	0	1	0	1		
	0	1	0	1	0	1	0	1	0	1		
	0	1	0	1	0	1	0	1	0	1		
	0	1	0	1	0	1	0	1	0	1		
	0	1	0	1	0	1	0	1	0	1		
	0	1	0	1	0	1	0	1	0	1		
	0	1	0	1	0	1	0	1	0	1		
	0	1	0	1	0	1	0	1	0	1		
	0	1	0	1	0	1	0	1	0	1		
	0	1	0	1	0	1	0	1	0	1		
	0	1	0	1	0	1	0	1	0	1		
	0	1	0	1	0	1	0	1	0	1		
	0	1	0	1	0	1	0	1	0	1		

Adapted from "South Carolina College- and Career-Ready Standards for Mathematics." South Carolina Department of Education. 2015. http://ed.sc.gov/instruction/standards-learning/mathematics/standards/scccr-standards-for-mathematics-final-print-on-one-side/.

Finally, the measures need to be efficient and easy to administer. You can design a checklist for determining skills over time and incorporate it into classroom center observations. (See "Mathematics Standards Checklist.") Similarly, systems such as a clipboard with a three-by-five-inch index card for each child on which teachers can record anecdotal notes (e.g., child's comments, questions), a folder with a sticky note for each child, or a tablet with a note-taking app can help you be systematic and efficient. Keeping track of each child's developmental level can help you know exactly which skills to scaffold for each child.

Step 3: Organize the Information You Collect

Once you have chosen the measures and begun collecting observations or samples of students' work, you need an efficient way to organize the information. First, make sure to date your records when you observe or take samples of students' work. Then, set up a simple strategy to quantify the information to help you summarize it. In the "First Grade

Writing Assessment" (page 130), Writing Processes and Applications contain four items. Therefore, you might assign each item 25 percent toward a total of 100 percent, representing mastery. Similarly, the "Mathematics Standards Checklist" illustrates a progression of math skills. You can sum up the number of skills mastered to date to get a total score—the higher the score, the more skills mastered in the progression. Designing a way to analyze each observation or to score each work sample can help you interpret the information. Additionally, you can record comments specific to each child's efforts. This method of data collection enables you to collect the range of documentation needed to make sense of your findings.

Your summaries are also useful for sharing students' progress over time with families. For example, showing a completed first grade writing assessment at a family–teacher conference at different times of the year could clearly illustrate a child's gains in essential areas of writing. Families can easily track and comprehend their child's progress and needs.

Step 4: Collect Information Across Time

Deciding when to gather data is an important decision. Teachers usually collect information on a goal or standard for the first time *before* instruction takes place to get baseline information and to see if any students have already mastered the learning goals about to be taught (*pre-assessment*). You can also collect information *during* a unit of instruction to see how students are doing and to determine what teaching strategies you might need to change to ensure that all students master the goals (*formative assessment*). For example, if you notice that several students are struggling with counting objects, you might devise a mini-lesson using concrete materials to supplement your instruction. You may also provide students with an exit ticket (e.g., students' written responses to questions posed at the end of a lesson) to quickly assess their understanding of the material you presented. These first two collection times are crucial for designing and adjusting strategies so that they are developmentally appropriate for the child. Finally, teachers usually collect information *after* the unit is complete to see whether all students mastered the goals. Often the end-of-unit assessment (*post assessment* or *summative assessment*) can involve additional elements that are more comprehensive than the initial assessment.

For example, in the math illustration measuring wood scraps with Unifix cubes, Mr. Edwards might decide to see which children exceeded the goal he set for their learning by asking more challenging questions at the end of the unit. To extend problem-solving skills and prompt thinking about measurement and numeral relationships, he could ask students to compare the lengths of two objects to determine which objects were the longest or shortest, use their operational skills to determine how many more units the longer object was than the shorter one, and illustrate how the objects could be ordered by length.

Step 5: Interpret the Assessment Results

When tracking children's progress across time, bear in mind important questions to guide your thinking about the data collected. Before instruction, one question is, "Have any students already mastered the standard?" If they have, you might need to increase the challenge of the unit. On the other hand, if many students have no items correct, you might need to check whether they have the prior knowledge needed for the unit. For example,

First Grade Writing Assessment

Name _____   Date _____

Pre-Score	Comments	Writing Processes and Applications	Post Score	Comments
0 1		Primarily draws pictures, but also uses a few letters to represent sounds of words to tell a story.	0 1	
0 1		Uses letters to represent sounds of words and invented spelling to tell a story, picture may accompany.	0 1	
0 1		Uses recognizable words to tell a story with a combination of invented and conventional spelling.	0 1	
0 1		Uses mostly conventionally spelled words to tell a story.	0 1	
		Writing Convention Indicators		
0 1		Uses uppercase and lowercase letters.	0 1	
0 1		Uses appropriate letter formation when printing.	0 1	
0 1		Capitilizes names of people.	0 1	
0 1		Places punctuation marks at the end of sentences.	0 1	
0 1		Uses commas to separate single words in a series.	0 1	
0 1		Uses correct sentence structure.	0 1	
0 1		Reads and understands own writing.	0 1	
	Total			**Total**

Adapted from Attachment A, "Check My Writing—Kindergarten." Ohio Department of Education. 2009. http://ims.ode.state.oh.us/ODE/IMS/Lessons/Content/CEW_LP_S01_BF_LKG_I07_01.pdf.

Adapted from "South Carolina College- and Career-Ready Standards for English Language Arts." South Carolina Department of Education. 2015. http://ed.sc.gov/instruction/standards-learning/mathematics/standards/scccr-standards-for-mathematics-final-print-on-one-side/.

when you look at a class profile on the "Mathematics Standards Checklist," you notice that the majority of students cannot count to 120 when measuring longer objects. Based on this assessment, you provide students with shorter objects to measure (e.g., up to 50 units) so that the task is developmentally appropriate.

After a formative assessment you might ask, "How many students made gains?" Then examine the students who have not improved and ask, "What types of problems are these students having?" Answering this question can help you design appropriate instruction to help these students close the gap between where they are and where they need to be.

At the end of a unit you might ask, "How many of the students mastered the learning goals?" Look for clues among students who did not master the goals, such as patterns in their errors. After interpreting and summarizing the assessment results, you can reflect on next steps to use with these students and changes to make the next time you teach this content.

To conclude the unit on measurement, Mr. Edwards and the students completed the "what I Learned" step of the **KWL** chart. Their responses included the following:

Quentin: My foot is sixteen Unifix cubes long and Daria's foot is fourteen Unifix cubes long. My foot is two cubes longer!

Jayden: Yeah, but Mr. Edwards's foot is the longest.

Felipe: Whose foot is the shortest?

Deidre: I want to measure my brother's foot to see if it is shorter than mine.

Gianna: Let's measure how tall Mr. Rockefeller (the school principal) is. I bet he is a thousand. Link 'N' Learn links long!

Wanda: I bet Mr. Edwards is taller than Mr. Rockefeller.

Isaiah: I used Color Tiles to measure the foot book we read. It was fifteen Color Tiles long.

Brianna: There is a bunch of cool stuff we can use to measure things.

Shaquia: I like the Measuring Worms the best!

Not only did the students master many of the standards Mr. Edwards addressed, but through their intense interest in measurement they acquired new knowledge, expanded their vocabulary, and were actively involved in their own learning.

Conclusion

Remember: Keep assessment simple. Focus on essential content. Assess before, during, and after you teach the selected content. Finally, assessments should address challenging, yet developmentally appropriate material, so students develop higher-order thinking skills. Assessment is essential for successfully pinpointing students' developmental level and fostering learning. It need not be complicated. Breaking assessment into the five steps described in this article will allow you to use continual, efficient assessments to ensure all students make progress toward mastering standards.

References

Ferguson, C. 2001. "Discovering, Supporting, and Promoting Young Children's Passions and Interests: One Teacher's Reflections." *Young Children* 56 (4): 6–11.

Green, S.K., & R.L. Johnson. 2009. *Assessment Is Essential*. New York: McGraw-Hill.

McTighe, J., & G. Wiggins. 2012. *Understanding by Design Framework*. www.ascd.org/ASCD/pdf/siteASCD/publications/UbD_WhitePaper0312.pdf.

NAEYC. 2011. "2010 NAEYC Standards for Initial and Advanced Early Childhood Professional Preparation Programs." www.naeyc.org/ecada/standards.

Smith, C.L., M. Wiser, C.W. Anderson, & J. Krajcik. 2006. "Implications of Research on Children's Learning for Standards and Assessment: A Proposed Learning Progression for Matter and the Atomic–Molecular Theory." *Measurement: Interdisciplinary Research and Perspectives* 4 (1–2): 1–98.

South Carolina Department of Education. 2015a. "South Carolina College- and Career-Ready Standards for English Language Arts." http://ed.sc.gov/scdoe/assets/file/programs-services/59/documents/ELA2015SCCCRStandards.pdf.

South Carolina Department of Education. 2015b. "South Carolina College- and Career-Ready Standards for Mathematics." http://ed.sc.gov/instruction/standards-learning/mathematics/standards/scccr-standards-for-mathematics-final-print-on-one-side/.

Vygotsky, L.S. [1930–35] 1978. *Mind in Society: The Development of Higher Psychological Processes*. Ed. and trans. M. Cole, V. John-Steiner, S. Scribner, & E. Souberman. Cambridge, MA: Harvard University Press.

Zimmerman, B. J. 2011. "Motivation Sources and Outcomes of Self-Regulated Learning and Performance." In *Handbook of Self- Regulation of Learning and Performance*, eds. B.J. Zimmerman & D.H. Schunk, 49–64. New York: Routledge.

About the Authors

Christine J. Ferguson, PhD, is professor of early childhood education and CAEP accreditation coordinator in the Department of Education at the University of South Carolina Beaufort, in Bluffton.

Susan K. Green, PhD, is professor emerita of educational psychology at Winthrop University, in Rock Hill, South Carolina.

Carol A. Marchel, PhD, is a professor in the Richard W. Riley College of Education at Winthrop University, where she teaches graduate and undergraduate courses in assessment, human development, and educational psychology.